MW00581869

SEMIOTEXT(E) Foreign Agents

© Editions Gallimard, Paris, 1980.
This edition Semiotext(e) © 2016

Published by Semiotext(e)
PO BOX 629, South Pasadena, CA 91031
www.semiotexte.com

Special thanks to John Ebert.

Design: Hedi El Kholti
Back Cover Photography by Jacqueline Salmon

ISNB: 978-1-58435-185-6
Distributed by The MIT Press, Cambridge, Mass. and London, England
Printed in the United States of America

THE ORDINARY MAN
OF CINEMA

Jean Louis Schefer

Translated by Max Cavitch, Paul Grant, and Noura Wedell

Contents

Preface   7

The Gods   25

Devil Dolls   27
The Mummy   31
The Jealousy of Freaks   35
Lost Horizons   37
The Inhuman Woman   39
The Maid on the Telephone   41
Occupation: Bouvard and Pécuchet   43
Laurel and Hardy: Brother and Sister   43
The Clown of Heraclitus   45
The White Orgy   47
The Black Orgy (The Slaves and the Painting)   49
The Object   51
The Shroud   53
The Sausage   55
Chickens   57
The Likeness   59
The Burlesque Body   60
The Death of Nero   63
The Death of Nero with a Character   65
The Phonograph   67
The ideal being can only be seen through the eyes of a criminal   69
From the Book of Satan   71
Burlesque 2   73
The Chubby One at the Theater   75
The Road Map   77
Nana   79
The Smoke   83
Shadows   85

In Front of the House   87
The Room   89
The Carriage, the Veins   91

The Criminal Life (The Film)   93

The Criminal Life   95
The Lesson of Darkness   121
The Wheel of Images   161
The Wheel   171
The Human Face   181

Translators' Notes   219
List of Photographs   223

Preface

Here, as the ordinary man of cinema, I would just mention something *inessential*: the cinema is not my profession. I go to the movies for entertainment, but sometimes while I'm there I also accidentally learn something, something different from what the film teaches me. (It will not teach me that I'm mortal, but it might show me a way of rediscovering time, or experiencing a dilation of bodies, and the unlikely occurrence of all this: indeed, rather than being a reader of films, I constantly remain their most submissive servant and their judge.) At the movies, I learn to be surprised at my capacity to live in many worlds at once.

I will thus speak here as a being without qualities.[1] All I want to say is this: I have no standing to speak about the cinema, except insofar as I spend a lot of time going to the movies. This habit has probably taught me something. Yes, but about what? About the films I see? About myself? About humanity? About memory?

What this "ordinary man" can say has less to do with a discourse (the transmission of knowledge) than with a kind of writing (a query of which the focus is the mystery, rather than the reconstruction, of an origin). The only origin of which I can properly speak—and discuss before you—is linked foremost to an elucidation of the visible. Not of its status, but of the certainty that it exists so strongly only because a world that is characterized as such opens within us, and because to some extent we ourselves are both the genesis and the fleeting life of that world, suspended to a totality of artifice.

What I've written here is that particular experience of time, of movement, and of images.

And yet I've held myself to certain theoretical premises. This book was never intended to be a theoretical essay on the cinema. It was never intended to do anything other than to give voice to that memory, to the show of its effects, and to lead it to a threshold of perception. I am in effect summoning a spectator's "knowledge" here. But it is *mine*, and so, inevitably, something of my life has transited here.

A machine turns, represents simultaneous action to the immobility of our bodies, and produces monsters: all this might seem rather more delicious than dreadful. Or perhaps, despite being in fact so dreadful, it is first of all an undeniable pleasure. Maybe it is the unknown, uncertain or shifting site of that pleasure, that nocturnal kinship of cinema, that prompts this questioning of both memory and meaning—questioning that, in our memory of a film, remains firmly attached to the experience of that experimental night during which something moves, comes alive, and speaks before us.

For the spectator, cinema is first and foremost something completely different than what filmic analyses reflect of it. The meaning that comes to us (and that comes to us inasmuch as we are a site of resonance for image effects, for the "depth" of images, and inasmuch as we handle the entire future of these images and sounds as affects and as meaning), that very particular quality of meaning made sensible is inextricably linked to the conditions of our vision; quite precisely to the experience (to the quality of that nocturnal experience that is the threshold of reception and the condition of existence of these images), and perhaps even to the very first experience of seeing them.

If the cinema—leaving aside for the moment its constant renewal in every film and in every screening of every film—is defined by its special power to produce lasting effects of memory, then we must know, and must have known for several generations, that through this memory a part of our lives passes into our recollections of films, including films that might seem totally unrelated to our lives' actual circumstances.

I thus wanted to account for that single feeling of persistent strangeness—as if it were that image-receiving humus—born with "my" cinema, and to write it down in order to make it palpable. For it is impossible that my experience of cinema could be completely solitary, for that's precisely the illusion proper to cinema, more so even than the illusion of the mobility of the objects we see on the screen. It is the illusion that this experience of cinema, this memory of it, is solitary, hidden, secretly individual, because it (this story, these images, these affective colorings) always seems to tie an immediate private pact with an unexpressed part of ourselves: that part given over to silence and to a relative aphasia as if it were the ultimate secret of our lives, when it is perhaps nothing but the ultimate subjection. Through this artificial solitude, it seems as if a part of ourselves is permeable to effects of meaning without ever being able to be born into meaning through our language. There, we even come to know—and to me this is the imprescriptible link between cinema and fear—an increase in sentimental aphasia in our social being. Cinema acts on every social being as if on a solitary being. The fear we experience at the movies (and this is every child's first experience at the movies, the one that colors all the rest) is not unmotivated, it is simply disproportionate. I've understood for a while that it inheres *in the fear* of this aphasic latency, because the latter has already cut into us so deeply.

I don't deny that there is pleasure in this. But I do want to clarify it somewhat (if only its ambiguity). In a word—and I am thus glossing over this entire book—this pleasure is no matter of straightforward enjoyment, or in brief, of aesthetic pleasure. It is, I think, the visual-experiential basis of all the pleasure we take in defining images—the basis, for example, of what we believe to be an "imaginative projection" into filmic action. It is the pleasure taken in our moral being, and that's why, to me, it's so close to its opposite: fear (which constitutes the highest point of simulating the realization of affects that are deprived of objects.) The reality of these feelings is the subjection to a world that derides them. I maintain that this can be called "experience," and that we can therefore speak about it seriously.

Suddenly, I attempt to recognize in these forms, on these collections of sounds and images in relation to which I do not intervene, and for whom I remain a spectator, what might be their essential counterbalance… in sum, to what void all form corresponds.

In unpredictable ways, all human forms (all imitations of a destiny) answer to the expression of the feelings that define our humanity, or to the necessity or basic overdue need to express those feelings.

It's not that we project ourselves onto forms or into beings, bearers of a part of identity that would be that part missing from all of life, or that would be the secret of what, since it does not stabilize into an image, keeps it alive outside of images. But the inexpressible also grows in the living as it lives, that is, it continually substitutes action to the possibility it has of contemplation in the void.

But these feelings, which rely upon the idea of a solitary profundity of the human, will be represented here solely *in the actions' body*. In order to sustain them, this body will have to be a new kind of thing so as to indicate the reflexivity of actions, not their power of transition, or their material resolution in the world. This reflexivity will of necessity augment the invisible world, that world in view of which an action properly occurs here (and through which an action is not an event there: such that the strongest capture of the image occurs in that world; all causality in that universe of images is locked into a body of enigmas, as if through a hint of signification.)

Perhaps a "being without qualities" such as myself will be permitted to state a truth here, to ask a question, and to make a claim. The aim would not be to bolster an image of the human according to theoretically determined structures. Instead, it will disrupt this image with quite deliberate unreasonableness by allowing contents to come to me (relations of contents and representations that are always quite precisely experimentations rather than representations).

If so, this is what must be understood: there is probably nothing theoretically salient to say about cinema that would, in the name of received wisdom about forms, confirm the social forms of anthropology. For cinema is a new kind of experience of time and memory, one that, alone, forms an experimental being.

Cinema doesn't compose or arrange a structure of alienation out of our participation in it. Rather, it creates a structure of realization and of appropriation of something that is real, not of something possible. The real in question is what already and momentarily lives as the spectator. That life is not a momentary and suspended life, but a memory of images and experimental affects: one must thus question the role of the script as the object, not of that person's desire for existence, but of their *fund of affects*. I say this without qualities.

In the same way: the oneiric structure of film is an anthropological delusion. And, if there still is some part of dream in film, it does not concern the fulfillment of desire. Rather, it *legitimates* desire, which is something much more essential.

There's nothing here that presupposes any specialized knowledge, just a certain habitual *usage of the invisible part of ourselves*—the part of us that needs to be taken up, taken in hand and into our own usage as it were. This part, which is without any sort of reflection upon us, is hopelessly given over to transforming its own obscurity into a *visible world*.

The only knowledge taken for granted here is that which comes from the *use* of our own memory: all it teaches us, ultimately, is how to manipulate time as image, made possible through the "subtraction" of our actual body.

This is not a response to some theory, but the acknowledgement of a simply paradoxical experience, an aporetic duration (the relation of an object of thought to what, in the very act of thinking, absents itself from thought). The experience itself is a source of aporias. Things no longer pertain to a hidden meaning, but to the difficult, vacillating relation between visible things and a secret that would be simply their own (it is thus ours, and like the photograph of our "body," without any resolution in the visible).

The duration of the passions (what Kierkegaard named the alternative to the lie of character)[2] can only be measured in the persistence of images—not, that is, by their duration in screen-time, but by their power of persistence, iteration, and recurrence. It is quite close to what defines their transformation into the image's anamnestic double, that is to say, into that kind of trace or back-up copy that would be internal to a slow movement of the disappearance or effacement of phenomena.

Cinema and cinematic images don't automatically call up any technical or theoretical knowledge. That kind of knowledge doesn't matter so much to me. And indeed cinema may be the only domain of signification in which no part of me can believe that the *operation of its science has a subject.*

Cinema is an art that awakens memory, in mysterious conjunction with the experience of a depth of feeling (but also a quite specific life of isolated affects). This is what resonates when Dreyer says: "What interests me—and this comes before technique—is reproducing the feelings of the characters in my films. That is, to reproduce, as sincerely as possible, the most sincere feelings possible... She had taken off her make-up, we made the tests, and I found on her face exactly what I had been seeking for Joan of Arc: a rustic woman, very sincere, who was also a woman who had suffered."[3]

This memory doesn't merely evoke, but writes an entire life's experience, as it leads away from the world. It is as if we went to the movies to progressively annihilate the film (on those few images we would retain of it) on the feelings we experience there, and then as if this mass of affects could progressively restore, in their light and affective coloring, chains of images.

I have been trying to explain how the cinema exists within us as a kind of ultimate chamber where the hope and ghost of an *interior history* circulate. Because this history does not unfold, and if it even occurs, can only remain invisible, without a face, without characters, and most of all, without duration. Through the persistence of their images, we acclimatize all the films we see to this absence of duration and of a scene where that interior history might be possible.

So there is this invisible chamber inside us, where, in the absence of any object, we torture the human race itself, and from which, mysteriously, incomprehensibly, the feeling or conscious anticipation of the sublime comes to us.

None of this clearly marks out the particular germ or anchor of feeling within a film. The film is perhaps nothing more than a kind of reflective surface that appears to us as such only at that precise moment when we are thrust away from it by the very feelings and affects it gives birth to: it does this only by simulating them in characters, in "bits of people" who have to die in order to ensure the continuity of what's beyond them.

Sight, in this way, makes me take leave of myself—that is, take leave of that most uncertain center of myself. Sight pushes it to find semblances of identity that chase it away like a center waiting to be surrounded.

So it's not exactly a commodity (some sort of sexual commodity), nor is it what you might call a pole of projection that I find when I go to the movies. I just find affects playing out a certain kind of scene—really, they're hardly what one would call feelings, just the stirrings of feelings linked to impossible actions, affects without intended objects, without a world, for no world preexists their affective coloring. In their unbreakable alliance, they play out their scene as the *visible interior of a species*. To the extent that it's the spectacle of *a visible human* (though not of course any particular embodied structure of recognizable pleasure, but some unknowable being), all it gives us to understand is that affects are a world, that is, are possibilities of actions occurring elsewhere, and, as such, are an inescapable destiny.

Could I, in good conscience and with a little clearheadedness, reduce the purposiveness of cinematic technique to the mere mechanical production of effects? What need? All of the simulations played out here already do the work of revealing their imperfection, or simultaneously show themselves to be simulations more or less equivalent to the mechanical production of effects. No, in this world, what I find compelling isn't the perfection of its illusions, but rather its illusion itself, and the fact that I can never reach the center of that illusion. This is because its illusion has no proper center, but is instead a mechanism for the elision of objects. There, in sum, bodily movements are not free; they are the spectacle that freedom has been deprived of. I will never reach the center of that illusion, moreover, because its world is composed by affects, not signification (which is simply the delay of affective relation): a world that is anterior, one that subsists without its proportions having been borrowed or appropriated from the real. By a basic alchemy, objects become prestigious only because they are rare (selected) and ancillary. They compose our cinematic universe, not through their easy resemblance to the things we've actually touched, seen, and coveted, but because they are woven of material altogether different. We desire them because they are a destiny: the dressing gown in *Little Caesar*, Fred Astaire's top hat and cane; Ketty's watch in *They Live by Night*, the dial of which is never seen but which nevertheless tells us the untimely hour of that nocturnal love and of the curse that weighs down upon the adolescents imprisoned by an ancient crime forever lodged into the shadow of their lives; Cary Grant's suit, which is his shield against knowledge of danger and attendant fear (I mean by this not to project an image of a sovereign consciousness but rather of a body in disguise, dressed first and foremost in the prismatics of minor passions, in sequences of gestures, words, and lighting).

The body (or the situation) is only desirable via the hope that it might hold what sheathes it, but also, and simultaneously, that its sheath would carry away with it all the worldly light in which it has been bathed. Did the nascent hallucination in which we ourselves began to repeat various gestures (for example, Eric von Stroheim's tics in *La Grande Illusion*) manage to induce in lieu of our bodies, like a gauzy chimera, the same rigidity as that of the actor, the same pleasure in detail, or to teach us that the cinematic body is a body that, like the old man in Bichat who "dies piecemeal," lives piecemeal?[4] What we could never recreate was the singularity of a world residing in transitions between gestures. It was striking, for example, that action could take place simply through the initiation of movement: someone might never be able to run away, yet their act would be complete, because at that moment, the whole world would necessarily become the entire consciousness of their flight such that nothing of the act could escape signification (and their flight might perhaps even be the singularity of that universe). And yet, endowed with a mobile structure, altered by shifting causalities, *it is neverthe-less just a mere intention of a world.*

And the burlesque—wasn't it simply the hypertrophy of a salient detail of our lives—or something we could get to know such that it would in its aggrandizement become the only meaningful detail, like the perpetual life of a fold of skin, or a silly hat always on the same head, or a leg in a permanent cast? There is in burlesque a kind of reflexivity and perception of action that really digs at a body and determines the way it appears. This is why burlesque is frightening: these bodies are already more guilty than clumsy, they are nothing but a light, gesticulatory reprieve as we wait for hell.

The world and its shadows rise up before our eyes, initiating us in the experience of undetectable movements.

The two trees the camera shoots from a distance, around which it begins to pan and to compose the incomplete panorama of which they are successively the center and the periphery—this group of trees in *Fortini/Cani* isn't simply composed of trees. This is not because those trees are simply a reflection of themselves, but because the distance from the world that we shall never reach subsists upon them. And this bouquet of trees doesn't simply preserve all the distance of the world. These trees, caught in a slow and brusquely sublime movement, are unnamed and unknown affects. They are that kind of silent, rigid, and delicate circumnavigation of the most unknown feeling. And why—if not because this scene suspends all movement within us—do we understand only that it is sublime?

In *Eureka*, Edgar Allan Poe depicts the genesis of matter, in which atoms apportion themselves by force of attraction and repulsion, and the soul is the product of repulsion.[5] Similarly, it is the unconsciousness, the misrecognition of this system of the luminous dots riddling bodies and encrusting faces that attends the birth of sentiments unrelated to our lives. Similarly, it is blindly that we enter into this world across a bridge of trembling light. Films are not chiefly constituted by more or less perfectly realized scenes, nor by visible, acknowledged stage settings (like those in *A Streetcar Named Desire*, which are theater sets filmed in close-up), nor by perspective points and shifts that reveal them to me. None of this is either credible or implausible. This world, beyond the artifice of its settings and its shots, before which I may remain incredulous, and which therefore can get away with being poorly made, doesn't settle me into the truth of a story. For it has already introduced me into the commingled truth and strangeness of affects that are whole and new—and dominating, because their quantities are novel, and because their object relations are novel as well.

I don't believe in the reality of film (its verisimilitude is unimportant), and yet for that reason I am in its ultimate truth. That truth is verified in me alone, not through any final reference to reality; it is, first of all, simply a shift in the proportion of the visible whose final arbiter I will no doubt be, as its body and experimental conscience.

There is no assurance added to this, the way a line might complete a more perfect image of a solid; what is added is the unsettling of the human voice (and perhaps only the doubt that it signifies). From this voice I retain certain qualities, a smoothness, a roughness, an exceptional composition—as was astonishingly realized by Michel Simon in *La Chienne*—and I only hear, behind its memory, the feeble burbling, the incoherence, and what seems the pathetic monologue of a lover's protest. Neither of the two voices, whether it belongs to Michel Simon or to Janie Marèze, is "real," that is, "reproduced." They are simply the truth of the scene. Whereas the voice of Janie Marèze is that of a type (it is "calibrated" to the historical depiction of a social class, attached to the irony of all the characters that borrow it, the irony of the "type"), the voice of Michel Simon is not that of a class, but is an invention, a blend that begins to constitute the volume level of his character. It is revealed in the scene of their conversation, in the sharing of the untenable secret that precedes the murder. Simon's vocal texture is alone in carrying that "culture that allows him to seem like an imbecile in his own milieu." In it I hear the beginning of that mocking tone which is always detectable in the voice of this actor, and which is the underlying, performed nature of his voice, that strange, old woman's quivering through which a feeling is always relayed, along with the *proper distancing* of the voice from the role, from the dialogue, as well as from the body of the actor himself. One hears the sibilants and dentals that characterize the "accent" of Protestant Geneva (the actor's birthplace), and the texture and composition of this voice play out in the character (Monsieur Legrand) as nostalgia for a place to which he has never belonged. The quivering voice and the rising accent rapidly lend him the air of a lunatic. As if listening to an opera, I can faintly hear what the voice itself signifies, the protest it makes through the sheer instrumentality of singing, which, even at the height of its artifice, cannot disguise the dazzling truth of the body, of the sudden apparition of that *visible human*, trembling like a wet dog.

The Gods

Devil Dolls

It is not because we are large that this woman seems small, but because we are *perched*, or on a turning pillar.

And perhaps we track this smallness under the feet of chairs, tables, blocks, or in the angles of shadows. Because the cross cast by a shadow on the path of this woman irremediably bars this path.

The shadow is nevertheless not the first thing one sees. It is here the contrasting and the secondary cause that makes the smallness evident—yet the tiny body is always grasped in its ideal perception. Her "dwarfism" must be divined (deduced) from the gigantism of the toys (giant children have abandoned the space, have abandoned these blocks as memories or traces of large couplings in their world).

The shadow, the proportions, the bodies inhabit precisely a world without strangeness. Here, it is given as a giant cube, illustrated with stories on its faces.

One does not imagine in what one sees here a reduction of the human figure but the absent children who are giants and who let this young woman flee, as if she were a subtle desire or an eel, she who will leap slightly to avoid a puddle.

More than to its fiction (the fantastic), the film and this image begin to introduce us to a constant truth of cinema: they entail two dimensions, that of bodies and objects, which may be unsynthesizable or which live separately. Common sense or the cinematographic habit tells me that their relations are "economic," that a close-up and a montage economize the plot, the description, and the action at the same time (it may be the sudden revelation of a cause, of an intention, or of an imminent action, or the instrumental withholding of an action). It teaches me that a universe of acts transitions through objects and that for characters, what motivates the plot may be the unconsciousness of this force of action latent in things (this is the function of a world of clues alongside the ignorance inherent to roles in film noir). The implacable destiny of the action also depends constantly on these objects being *already counted*, and on this infinite limitation being the first meaning that characters in film noir will only understand by ceasing to speak, by reproducing that initial arrangement that their actions have disturbed, in sum, by turning their steps back to the beginning of the film. Whatever Tod Browning is doing in *The Devil-Doll*, it is certainly not the simple reversal of these two proportions. Nonetheless, in addition to the characters and the objects that they inhabit (that is to say, a world of predicates: any object can be added to a body) or that they handle (like weapons: each object is a threat because it contains the truth of a behavior) a sort of supplemental pole appears: there are objects smaller than objects, and these are bodies, or the latent knowledge (the exclusive awareness of pitfalls) of a loss of control over the world of actions. These bodies might in turn touch even smaller objects if they weren't the *lost body* of the characters of a prior drama. At the culmination of each of their acts, reduced to pure quantities of action and improbable conduct, is always this virtual pole of images of action that can only uncover clues like so many blocks of granite.

Now I don't know why a woman would attempt this ultimate escape (or this exploration?); assuredly it's because she cannot be both a toy and the consciousness that we have of it.

The Mummy

Cinema's creatures are thus meant to scare us—which is to say, to create the conditions for a sudden internal shift in proportionality in us (and is not fear an event that is just as sudden as the change of our interior world, a change that does not alter the exterior forms among which we'd been living until then without concern—as if this alteration set in motion a series of figures that are impossible to copy within us and that exist at a far remove from our spirit.) Something becomes unhinged in the symmetry of objects, which in the end does not alter our images but shifts the repose that we can find in them—or that we hoped to find in them, in that act that takes us fully out of ourselves.

Cinema is thus that paradox as well.

Here arises a being that was never engendered in this world (nor in history); an organism endemic to cinema comes to infect us with its impossible birth. And as a spectator I am thus the perpetual site of this birth and of a duration that is never granted to monsters. The monster, in his grotesquery (always a clumsy amalgam of various mythologies that, in itself, never produces any effect) bestows degrees of reality

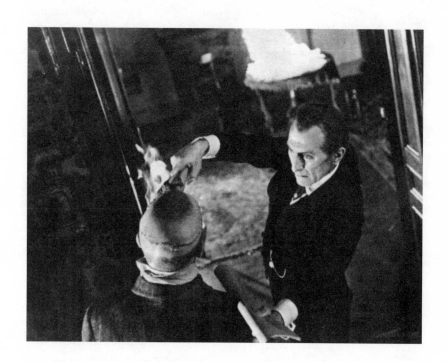

upon those he menaces. This mummy, giant puppet of rags and wrappings, covered in an armor of pus, bestows, even through blindfolded eyes, the gaze of putrefaction by which the world is condemned. He does not speak, he moans. It is because, at that instant, he is the unremitting pain of our perforated brain that we let him destroy the world.

This does not begin in horror, not even in fear. Upon this body covered in tatters, this body that is simply the bearer of all the bandages of our lives, of our entire hospital life, the world of pain takes a step that shrinks the entire ceremony, that is, our entire education. Such affects (these tortured beings) are uninhabitable, they are compensated by nothing: they are nothing but bodies.

Look at this puppet, defiled by nothing other than the duration of suffering it is condemned to express without pause. It is you climbing back out of that cave. It is you who feels the searing of the brandished torch in the back of your head. It is you—or you without the power to endure.

Is it the body of our enemy that the mummy folds over its knee? What protrudes from that pile of clothes is a snout, a kind of foreshortened trunk: it represents no one.

The Jealousy of Freaks

To me comes the fearful impression that the worst sufferings are silent.

Here, we were supposed to experience (is this the intention of the film or is it merely a parade of monsters according to a random script?) that there are affects—emotions, sorrows, rages—proportionate to the size of their subjects, reduced here to the foot-stamping (that is to the tiny movements) of dwarves' feet, to puny clenched fists, to miniscule tears. But such emotions, because of this uniformly reduced size, pass beneath us, provoking all the same state of repulsion: we do not inhabit such bodies because their voices are insufficiently audible, pitched too high to make us truly blanch, and because in the end we do not dwell in their anguish, which, even in the case of heartbreak, is nothing more to us than the fate of painfully little dolls.

This is ghastly, it is the worst sort of horror, but such is our truth that we inhabit bodies first and foremost without sarcasm. How can bearers of a sublime suffering, those who discover all the pain in the world, without adding in us the atrocity that deadens true grief and without wounding their true suffering by their expression, escape this place of tragedy when they can't even reach the doorknob? The meaning comes later, after this instability of affects in very small bodies. It is already there when we ask: "Why is our hell so small?"

Lost Horizons

This world is not symmetrical, it is transparent.

A lethal silence reigns here; even the money, which I imagine this mixture of Hollywood bathrooms and Arabian palace gardens is meant to suggest, vanishes like footprints in the desert. This edifice—and this garden, the most abandoned in the entire universe, accommodating neither complaint nor sigh—gives no impression of pleasure: it is smoothly symmetrical and transparent, as if placed in the midst of these many reflections. No one would have the impudence to suffer in such a place.

This mystery does not excuse our existence, but slips our impossible body into it without placing it anywhere. Are we the son of the chimerical potentate who built the palace where rain could fall, or the empty-headed daughter of the capricious tyrant, who has amassed his wealth in this glass confection and this uninhabitable crystal. Thus by despairing of ever using the image of this fortune, our actor's life is barred from this scene. No swarm of flies foreshadow Oedipus here, no insect drones. It can only rain endlessly: clearly we are not there.

This palace, truncated by the frame, rises to its height in the water of a pool; this is why this symmetrical world is merely transparent and why these columns, these railings whose only disproportion is their repetition, this world with no outside cannot collapse (it is too fragile for that; the pool cannot reflect any other image than those straight lines); this chimera, this edifice without a scale will not disappear; it will keep running and trickling endlessly beyond us. There isn't a fly that can mar it.

It is just as understandable that that this colossal sugar-works could endlessly shrink before our eyes into a miniature of itself in a shop window.

The Inhuman Woman

This man in hat and overcoat wore tinted glasses like Robespierre[6] out of fear of the incessant raids of beetles that had been attacking eyes for a year. These same glasses constantly prevented him from seeing shadows. He could as a result distinguish all geometric forms and the bodies of objects solidified and aspirated by a light whose reverse-shot he erased through an optical illusion, erasing its opposing source, which is to say, duration. The tinted glasses were thus destined to protect all objects from a light that emanated from the eyes, which would have irradiated them and rendered them flattened shadows.

In the same way, the worker busy on the roof removing his shadow from a wall removes only a pile of leaves, fallen at the base of the building.

If this man is blind, he has just groped his way into the scene to delay the beginning of the invisible story that will unfold there. At that point, he'll take off his glasses, his coat, and his hat, and the radiance of the theatrical bodies will whiten our eyes.

The Maid on the Telephone

The maid is obscene. He is submissive and impossible to break: he is already dead. This animal is more supple than a dog, more durable than a camel, and more elastic than a weasel, simply because he has never woken up.

Thus, there is what the script calls for (this gag), which appears here as if by chance: the maid on a platter, the latter being the maître d' of a makeshift hotel; and in this unequipped kitchen what could one make other than bodies that use the phone in paradoxical positions? But is there really an orthopedics of the telephone? And so the burlesque informs us: there exists a spelling of inactive bodies—not only inactive, but also having no position in space and activating nothing in turn: they are immobile. Normal movement would be nothing more than a category of the most absolute rest. It is thus the entire body, rather than the contingency of its psychology, that is a fiction. And if I linger another moment in this kitchen, what can I do? Undo the girl's apron, count the ceramic tiles, measure the improbably high placement of the telephone and become the smallest Lilliputian of all? And will I, because of all this, weep and shrink?

Occupation:
Bouvard and Pécuchet

Is it a genuine relief to learn that Laurel and Hardy are not homosexuals but rather a pair of male mothers-in-law condemned to live together?

Like Bouvard and Pécuchet,[7] these two lads recreate something that can never be *accomplished* (and their entire lives are an effort to perfect this incomplete past): adolescence.

Or it could be this: two lads trying with bodies that lack credibility to recreate adolescence, and who are fatally trapped by the curse of being two mothers-in-law in drag.

They're simply two old bachelors who are married. But whom else could they be married to?

Is this why, behind these faces, this fat, big-bottomed lad (who nevertheless has a mouse-mustache) and this other pale, cardiac phantom, and the gestures of those gloved hands through which every object in the room comes to stick to them, there's such anxiety in our amusement? Not only because the film is so consistently beyond them or so far from them, but also because these two cretins who suffer no mutilations, afflict us with their life, this face to face, and these somewhat edifying and yet simplistic jokes? The film couldn't

begin because of them, so it would have been good to know when it was going to end—that is, in short, with whom they were married.

Laurel and Hardy:
Brother and Sister

It's a big surprise (they so often go home dirty or drunk) to learn that they have young and pretty wives.

Yet they are condemned to interchangeable feminine roles (not by means of their activities, which, to be honest, are mysterious and consist mostly of clumsily undoing one thing or another): pouting, beaten-down women. They are, in relation to one another, a young couple (there is this emotion in their disgrace: how to face the world and present themselves together?); but nonetheless, there is nothing between them but the relationship of mothers-in-law.

But isn't it the same thing that amuses us, that troubles us, or at least make us dream of this kind of imitation in the useless science and impotent knowledge of Bouvard and Pécuchet, as if this blockage and reciprocal parasitism of actions and speech spread out, behind them and before us, the feverish language, the words before the words of a kind of incomprehensible science? That together they were only the illusion of an embryonic author.

The Clown of Heraclitus

— I'm looking for something!
— Did you lose something?
— Yes!
— Did you lose it here?
— No!
— Then why are you looking here?
— Because there's light here!

Why is this less comic than poignant, and why is this absurdity immediately sublime? Will the thing lost in the shadows immediately appear in the circle of light where I seek it? And is it, as in the saying of Heraclitus, that every assertion about an object is but an expression of my passage through the world? In any case, never in this light will I find my shadow lost in the shadows.

The White Orgy

The most perfect body is an earth-worm, which makes it above all others susceptible to the most extreme weakening, making it both victim and perpetrator. And at that moment the orgy will be complete.

The bodies (the luxuriousness of the added whiteness, silk, and satin) are not destined to an out-burst or to a raging party. They must melt away little by little like pastries into their collective con-tact. In my view, an overheating of signs (luxury, eroticism, eccentricity, taste, a depravity) exhausts these poor little chicks: one of them was a man. But one doesn't triumph so easily over images. These bodies that touch don't exactly form a group, a heap, or a machine that swallows up riches (and thus a machine for representing expendi-ture and creation of money, nor the strangeness of this *money without poverty*). They also produce what the image alone reveals: a body resulting from all the touching of this white mass, slender legs, and curves. This little anatomy is able to cancel out all the others, as if, in this final judgment, there appeared the perfect hermaphrodite and the divine child, neither sighing nor dreaming. It's a puzzle, a sudden pinch, the solitary heart or the lonely nausea of all these powdered forms.

A ceremony during which no murder is committed and no body disappears is a scene. This scene is straightaway represented for the edification of families, and this, which the big girls of the house and their cousins play, is called a charade.

The Black Orgy
(The Slaves and the Painting)

According to Taine and Delacroix, the use of live models in Mannerism initiated a kind of decadence of the arts of the body.

The black slaves (and we are spared the pleasure of this) are chained to the painting they cannot reproduce: the nude against the wall is inspired by Correggio.

Meanwhile, a kind of "rotundity of signs," that which presides over this genre of composition, is shattered on this image. Is it because the Titian or Correggio nude must here move its legs to resemble those whites covered in shoe-polish, chained together (ridiculed) and who resemble torturers more than victims?

A kind of imprecision reigns in the image of this film, because nothing is added to it, because the supreme idea of luxury (eroticism, or the art of producing expenditure beyond measure) doesn't appear in the made-up faces and because this can't align itself with any order (with any class, or religion) and isn't even execrable.

This scene should therefore be amusing; it isn't even shocking (it stirs no conviction or scruple of mine), and it is so minimally shocking because it is dated or signed by trinkets (small columns, plaster cupids, glass baubles). These are not bodies that have been purchased; they *arouse* no suspicion, radiate no pleasure, have no care that they would jealously guard: they appear. An assembly of paltry cretins in a shared indigestion of chocolate, in which all its savagery resides.

The Object

Enigmatic objects (without attribution), modest attitudes and lowered eyes: it's a kind of pass-the-slipper game, interrupted by the same attitude at once modest and indecent. We must imagine the bottom, the owner of such knickers; here is the embarrassment and the relief of the whole approach, the owner of this piece of linen will have lowered eyes.

This is one of the most obscene photographs I know (I should thus explain the type of horror it reveals): none of the people here is exactly desirable but the group forms a rebus. It contains one of the largest asses, of which Hardy distastefully holds the proof.

One is thus at a kind of border, at the front, in the trenches. Cinema's ideal body (the hero or other medium of a sublime desire) cannot enter here. The entire scene, and the scene's front, is occupied by mothers-in-law.

Here Laurel and Hardy disclose something of the permanence of all their roles (we see what they show us, brilliantly, because we are never their accomplices).

Thinking back on this vast displacement, I recall the sequence from a Stroheim film[8] in which the young cavalry officer he plays passes a parade of boarding school girls and, with the tip of his saber, notices or points to a student's underwear, which has fallen about her ankles (this is sublime, why? because this causes the young girl to fall in love with him?). The same audacity propels these two scenes, through the scarcely dangerous public display of these empty drawers, from the moment these pieces of evidence fall, not as pockets or sacks, but as matter, as *scraps of questioning*. In the Laurel and Hardy scene, a combination is conceivable yet impossible; each anatomical grouping, that is each couple, whispers a secret about the other—one doesn't question the fashion of such strange pantaloons in the hands of a man (he doesn't offer them up, or handle them devotedly, or sniff them); one asks not who will get them but whose they are.

This obscenity is a miracle of signification. This fabric cut for two legs could pass just as easily beneath the noses of these characters as if it were on a piece of wire. Something is exchanged among this group that is not clumsiness or rudeness: in the manipulation of this intimate garment, indiscretion ceases from the moment we hold not a garment but a sex.

The Shroud

Something here does not match up: the laundry, the light, the shadows, the gate which guides us toward the light, the ancient squalor (is this from poverty, humility?) that like a kind of fate leads our eyes toward the flash, the cloth, laundered before our very eyes, and which has begun—as faraway as we are—to place the veil of a shroud upon our chest. It's not quite a screen that this woman extends towards us, and that arrests, to slow down any wild beast, the innocence and the light without image. It is an uncorrupted light because it has no source, or because the gesture of lifting it produces its cause: an immaculate flash, a lucent duration, an entire world of snow could conjure in us both a horizon and a cause. And is it not also sublime because the dirty cloth chosen from our laundry basket is, incomprehensibly, nothing other than the advent of a suffering for which, through the repetition of this arrested gesture, I must recreate the insurmountable entryway within myself. Leaving us sitting in the night, in that which grows taut, and that cloth without memory, without image or shadow, rises and rustles endlessly beneath our eyelids, nourishing us—because nobody moves here and no fly sullies it—but it nourishes us with this white shadow, which arrives here beyond the world.

I imagine no other scene than this one, in a loop, completed in this infinite repetition that would last a lifetime: this woman bends down, chooses this sheet, and we alone, by these hands, this kindness, and this pity must become the whiteness, the sheet, the breeze that dries it, and the incomprehensible entry-point of a light that will prolong an entirely different night.

But you yourself will never again dance to the projection of your shadow, of your memory, or of any past on this miraculous surface. We understand much later that shadows massing and still divided, streaked, and also gliding through dust, will never achieve this flash. Because through them alone a story also transits, with an adventure and screams—because, in the end, this shadow repeats words within us, and in every corner whispers memories, that is, shadows.

Does a new man breathe in me? It's this rag, this shroud shining without imprint, that no one dares touch.

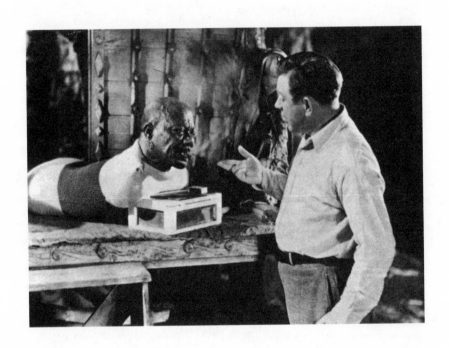

The Sausage

Is this still a man, or already a monster? Is a man somewhere other than in his face, that is, where he can be equally sublime and heinous? I don't know why this character in *Freaks* reduced or condensed into a sole, swaddled member (a member and not an organ), reduced into this creeping muff that the photograph shows us, evokes the Husserlian idea of the curious subtraction of phenomena giving access to essences.

This being reduced to a member and to an action (who shows us his skill in the film, that is, assures us of his humanity by lighting a cigarette), in his slithering and his odd batting of a monstrous tail (in truth the progressively watchable horror—and only because he completes an action—of a disproportionate penis joined to a pirate's head), threatens the last vestiges of humanity in us. This sideshow performance (this unnecessary demonstration submitted as proof) just barely deflects our attention to a more unsettling question: what can such a sausage do, not with his desires or his dreams, but with his excrement? And does this sweater hide for the entire film the fact that his arms are actually folded, squeezed, and temporarily miniaturized and that this buccaneer will eventually stretch and yawn? Is it also because we feel our own limbs tighten and our arms stick to our bodies? What could possibly be the fate, which is to say the duration, of such an animal? And why is his matchbox placed on this miniature aquarium?

And do they stuff a cigarette in his mouth to keep him from screaming, so that he doesn't have time, for the duration of his life on film, to speak to us or even to address a word to the thing in us which is precisely "that"?

Thus we are "that," and in this aging larva's life—a buccaneer who over the course of his battles progressively lost all of his limbs to the sword, and who wrapped himself in this enormous mariner's cap (and what mother could have knitted such a thing?)—we tremble to imagine and to comprehend that this tube we see inhaling smoke has experienced the sorrows of love? And is that the monster: perpetual heartache and its animal groans?

I'm not sure why this little pedestal, along with the objects placed in front of him, inspires in us the idea of the public writer?

Chickens

Why should they be large fowl, decked out for this feast, this wedding, with plumes at the center of their heads, rendering them idiotic? We have abandoned the bodies of prehistoric animals only by losing various organs of sight and sound, incalculable capacities for crawling, vibratory antennae, exceptional extensions of nerves, gills, an immense compulsion, and an extraordinary power to crawl. And this banquet of cretins is an assembly of monsters, not because we spawned them, but because they have been transformed far more quickly than ourselves. They are here not to eat, perhaps mostly to drool, but because they await their world, and because that world struggles to be born—what is this horror? Their gestures and bearing make these fowl imitate a world they don't know, where nothing is their size, where no movement of the arm precisely touches all points in a sphere of movements. For example, the being who dances on the long table is lighter than a seguidilla dancer, yet she runs the risk of growing wings, of flying away, cackling, or of swimming below the ocean at lightning speed: she would have cousins the world over, probably twins. And yet she possesses only our dreams, and her twirling immobilizes us (it's her only sadism, in addition to her appearance). Why is she more horrifying than that dancer sculpted by Degas, dressed today in rags and lifting a nose or snout toward the sky? It's because she doesn't trace a surprising state of movement; she commands our immobility beneath that step that hammers out something in us and forces it to recoil.

The Likeness

If the "day in the country" is a genre, then is this not a pinnacle of the genre? These two species of geese who have no idea how to "adapt" their eyes would be (just like all their kind) the metaphor become visible, transformed into a species, tall awkward girls, a bit dopey and poorly put together—I can always imagine seeing a couple of provincial cousins crop up who look like this.

This picture, which does, after all, comply with the rules of an art—since all that is necessary is that it be a composition, that it organize characters and poses, and arrange the scenery—is perhaps troubling due to the very excess of its accessoriness. It's not implausible, but—more than all painting where the figure appears only because it has already been deformed in order to appear—likeness itself.

Does it resemble because it horrifies us, or because we recognize it? And we recognize it in that we aren't in it yet; otherwise we couldn't identify it, and *it would be the one to choose us.*

Is its resemblance something ineffably enclosed within itself? This world—and this is its madness—endlessly resembles itself; that is its horror.

More than abnormal men and women, we see slightly eccentric animals in these endless childhoods. I was forgetting that strange elongated fowl playing music in the foreground. Is this man too skinny to be eaten? Can he no longer support himself on these frail legs? And is his destiny to be carried from stretcher to stretcher to his ultimate emaciation? Will he attempt to charm three idiotic vampires with his instrument, or has he already transformed other monsters into this trinity that is beaming through its impotence? The amputee is the only one who conveys something of Signorelli's *Last Judgment*, which is to say a color added to the interior of the scene.

Of course, none of this points to anyone outside of the image, yet neither does it manage to show us "others"; relentlessly, in solitude even to the sound of the flute in this hideous countryside, a likeness is enclosed here.

The Burlesque Body

The burlesque body is mobile, malleable, transfusable, like the real context of the film's adventures. And in such weak scripts, the body is the first site and the first object of action—that is precisely why the latter is not dramatic. Dramatic action takes as its object souls and consciences. Its object is thus what is not represented, yet what also demands narrative complexity in the script, and forces characters to turn all of their flesh away from an action, or allows them to be something else than its simple avatar.

It is a constant that burlesque adventures avoid the development of a story and only achieve the "figure" of characters. These are not yet gods; nothing in their faces or their frumpy clothes gives a hint of the majesty of the great actors of film noir. They are given over to a fate (reducible to an action sequence) that transforms, undresses, sullies, and never idealizes them, never advancing their story in the slightest. There is no divinity reigning over their lives with which they could trade places (as happens later with the Bank, the Press, and Fame).

Here an unknown is substituted for this story-ruling divinity that is fatality or tragedy (but "before" the birth of tragedy and as if before the invention of speech): here, the body is experimented on, and subjected to variation.

Thus during the burlesque era the actor's body contains no modules, because it is not a vehicle for action (what we might "desire"—that is, understand—in the heroes of tragic cinema is not their physique. Rather, it is the sublime fatality of which the body is the intangible and incomprehensible vehicle). Before becoming characters, they are types—that is, the very matter of action. But this matt-like effect (which relies little on the effect of close-ups, because there is little need for detail beyond the narrative) is irreversible: they are merely bodies, which is why they are singular, inassimilable, and generating no desire to take their place. These types don't compose classes but humankinds: this is how instead of wanting to be in their place or in their role in the story, one could only "imitate" them—inhabit some aspect of their bodily gestures, because they are expressionless. "To do Chaplin," for example; even though Chaplin was a completely different case, aging and being transformed over the course of different scripts. Fatty or Hardy didn't age: they simply maintained their bodies until the

end and simply died before our eyes in the same condition, still as far from us, but not unlike the stuffed animals of our childhood.

An incomprehensible tenderness, albeit one that stems from no memory, attaches us to these men. And yet we have never been with them; they have never inhabited us. They are the perpetual witness and ancient gaze of one of our ages. It must be, paradoxically, that something of our own knowledge is in

them and that we charge them—more than our unfinished and now nearly invisible childhood—with everything we learn. And do those men dwell in us like Mentors, witnesses to what doesn't change in what we add to ourselves?

The Death of Nero

A gray whisper covers this image because this character performs—*emits*—the revelation of a secret he does not pronounce. We do not hear the words of this revelation, such a revelation that would assure us of the identity of this character. The silence inhabited unstably by this character assures us that a place of action exists somewhere else (its parenthesis and suspension are played out here), where the drama's decisive act unfolds while we are watching this, or that in what we are not watching there exists an even more malevolent character.

Here, the whispering between the acts (it's an ancient tragedy with Nero moving toward the bushes; it's an obscure Japanese film,) reveals only the span of a Shakespearian prologue, and this is not a character but an actor.

It is an actor who accomplishes before our eyes the possible truth of a role. He is also not endowed with sentiments because we must decipher him among the unending grayness of toga folds, undergrowth and stones. The burlesque scene from which he is separated is impossible for us to guess at, and irretrievable, and yet the drama that he does not express passes into him as he purses his lips as if to whistle or to breathe in the scorching air. He simpers in the body of a compulsive habitué of pastry or tearooms. And yet despite the graininess of the image, we know he is whispering roles to us—separated from us by an invisible stone wall, he has been the dying Nero, he has witnessed the disaster of Pompeii. Yet only this must we understand: this transvestite, this pastry cook can do nothing more than brush his lips with the names of these tragic moments of antiquity.

The Death of Nero
with a Character

This one just performed the death of Nero. Is he this surprised because beneath his feminine disguise he is looking for a lost word, or the beard he forgot to put on, or the two things absent from the servant's tray, the fatal absence of which reveals an imminent catastrophe?

Is this a writer without a book, one who will never write a novel? We surprise him at the moment he was about to talk about himself, after having made himself up as a woman, or in the act itself by which...

Nero, finishing his make-up in his dressing room before appearing on stage, receives a telegram announcing the failed attack on Agrippina, or that Tacitus is in the audience.

Or even Judith and Holofernes. Judith doesn't have her double-edged sword and Holofernes simply becomes a woman.

The Phonograph

So there exists music that can be played underwater. Even if this water is completely black [black because it's enclosed in this barrack, because the catastrophe or diversion that has flooded this room, and transformed these bedframes into houses on stilts, soaks up the notion of stains, dejections, scattered laundry which attend our residence or our sleep in a closed space—we soil a great deal (our kind is constantly soiling all kinds of laundry because we don't eat our own excrement), and in the past these men of early cinema were always leaving spit and tobacco juice at their feet]. This water sweats and drips the exhaustion of these unknown characters like grease. It is also the effect of an absolute absent-mindedness. If we saw the water rising amid these soldiers' snores, it's that they were only surprised by sleep.

We will thus have to live eternally in this new space and this scenography of flooding contained in a soldiers' barrack. Is this the whole of burlesque, or its law: the action is obstinately normal, simply stubborn in a polymorphous universe, because the latter consists only of the unfolding of elements and because cosmic order can be measured by a turbulence that is contained in a single room. It is there that the high tides will take place, that thunder will rumble, that it will rain flour, or that the earth will tremble—because it is there that the light will first decompose. Chaplin, for example, has us witness that he acts appropriately, in keeping with what he had learned a while back. Yet he didn't know certain things about the placement of objects around him, or the consistency of matter, until a few seconds ago, although that was already another age of the world. Since then, the dust has become an ocean, the pots swim, and the chairs float, because, furtively, in his agitated sleep, one of the sleepers had to urinate.

Will this gramophone, whose speaker we see, be able to produce sounds, to replay melodies? Will it make the sonorous distance audible, give sound to the vague gap that separates two states of the world? And will it make audible as *a form* the sonorous world of a flood captive within walls, which is to say nothing other than the sonorous world of all silent cinema? Can this sound be anything other than the amplified echo of the dry snoring of the projector: the stuttering and jumping of the image? This sound, which will never arrive, returns to the image like the loop of burlesque movements. For the moment, it must swim.

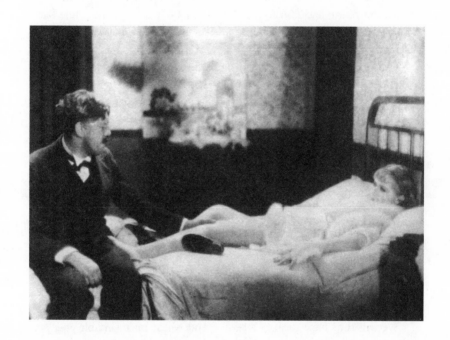

The ideal being can only be seen through the eyes of a criminal...

...because he desires (the age of psychology has shown us this) to perpetuate or to preserve photographically something that ought to remain fleeting. That flash must thus live on only as a memory (Renoir presents it to us as an image), saintliness in abjection, gentleness in cruelty. We may not see these words, or their reality, but we observe nevertheless the nimbus around the chosen victim, and are present to that whisper of love that cannot stir or *sway* this light (like the blinding form of God in the vision of Moses).

In the novel by Musil,[9] Moosbrugger killed prostitutes but could not kill horror or his desire, his complicity or his mother. Thus he touched eternity—fatally touched that which was always missing in himself (and why in that particular form?), missing unto eternity: the most obscure reason why no god ever wanted him.

And so it is thanks to this cliché of an old man, with his old woman's voice, that the scathing light of youth appears and lingers. We understand that an era is pushing him away, but that it was his own innocence and careless sense of pleasure that first killed him as a man. And thus it is in this much earlier death—accomplished long before her own murder—that "the bitch" must be enshrined in order both to lose and to retain her luminousness.

This splendor is not merely a look (or a desire, the coexistence of two images of the same body, both an object of murder and an inviolable body), it is the shear unreality of the world Legrand cannot penetrate: heavens *upon* "a bitch."

From the Book of Satan

The shadow is the mise-en-scène of a single point, of a stain and a flash of light. A few bodies are thus destined (almost criminally) to bear the light or to be borne away by it—to be but subtracted from the weight of shadows.

What lives in the image is still its fall, or the time during which something essential is suspended, until a kind of denial of its meaning (that would be its subterranean work) strikes us with this momentary truth embedded in it.

Thus the film's title, insisting that we find somewhere, or read here, a "leaf" torn from Satan's book. Is this body, inexplicably absorbed by the light it consumes, not that page from the middle of the book, and without its *verso*, the only leaf added to Satan's book? And that which makes the entire book an addition to that single leaf? And this precisely, if in this offering and gesture of luminous devotion, the body of a young girl weights only as much as the light that touches her and that she emits, out of a moment of endless purity—she will only be able to fade away through the shaft of a shadow.

Burlesque 2

These images aren't so much described as deducted from the relentlessness that uses them for their meaning, for what we retain from all these films. From that point they are wound upon around another time or on the scenario that unfolds in us (the image's novelty calls up an ancient knowledge that the film never elicited).

What happens to the characters is called a body and a fate (burlesque is defined this way: the character is the body's role; it can't escape this figurative mass for any action).

This body does not drive or guide actions. It absorbs them; it is the catastrophic, bursting site of their return, of their impossible liberation. These anatomies are also nothing but the world, this character but an actor. The movement to absorb and extinguish an action suddenly reveals to us a man—never women; women in burlesque are a difficulty added to the action; like a mirror, women refer the actors to a kind of "non-being" that is this particular, constant impossibility of "beginning" acts that remain the same. This, ultimately, is the genre's secret: it reveals an ageless adolescence, an eternality to these beginnings of the world in these stirrings of behavior. What, then, could be the perpetual subject of these comedies if not the real age of the spectators of these films, of which the charm is to toy a bit (like a psychoanalysis beginning with the same matter) with such arrested development?

It's also this implacable fate of a new beginning that assigns an age to each of its spectators—that age at which no action succeeds because it is nothing but anxiety, or an uncertainty about the body's purpose that acts. They are there, consoled incomprehensibly by a childhood; but they are instantly compelled, too, to repeat it, because they are not simple witnesses of the burlesque "mode."

But is this called a phantom, or a shadow? And how to pass this under the slightest approval: that this shadow is like all the bread, eaten and not eaten, cooked during this age?

And the sublime despair, as much as the unstoppable laughter at impossible actions, fills me with a horror of the simplest food, become a spongy stone, stuffed into the mouth it props open.

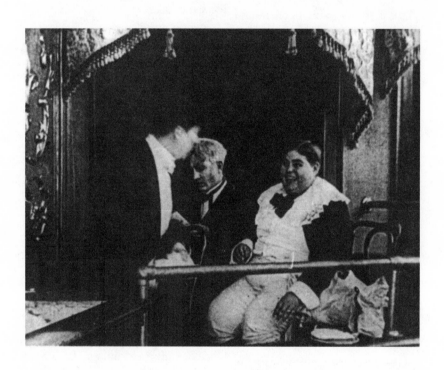

The Chubby One
at the Theater

Or at the music hall. There is in any case in the bloated first communicant who spills over the box like his buttocks over the chair something that rids us of those good stories of Lewis Carroll (of those children of mirages, trap-doors, and double-meanings!), of Bruno and also of Sylvie, of the boredom generated by these texts as soon as they are marked out for intelligent or industrious children. This jovial ass, this triumph of a duncish first communicant finally reunites the imagination of the gobbler of chocolate éclairs and the skinny pervert who pinches little girls' thighs at catechism. It's unlikely that one of us (or I myself) has been this boy, in spite of the large lace collar on a costume in which we would have heaved very different sighs. It is, in fact, the character from a painting, one of "The Children of Edward,"[10] the very model of the boy we want to haul off to the vaudeville show and stuff with sweets like a Buddha. It's Little Lord Fauntleroy[11] they made us read, so that we would become like him, just as lovely and melancholy—he simply ate the book, the soup, and the dessert of all the melancholy children. So it's

(was it already that way?) the revenge of our unaccomplished acts—of all the bottoms never pinched or the deprivations of dessert. The actor kept eating all the while.

There is no other incongruity: the model of the portrait roams at will, and this wandering is already a catastrophe. In all of this the actor aligns himself with perhaps one desire (a nostalgia) and its irony: to put on our childhood clothes today without ripping them and without their becoming cast-off rags, flapping on our other bodies despite their smallness. This film, like all burlesque, is nevertheless not a parade of monsters, because we would become without delay the memory of such monsters. It is nonetheless made in its entirety not to go beyond what it shows: this body, for example.

The Road Map

The Buster Keaton film presented this image only in a fugitive way; it gave only its installation, not its condition or duration.

Thus it is here a completely different field and a kind of compensation of the script (and this loss of image that is narrative possibility) of which the following is given to us. This is duration seized fantasmatically by an immobile body; such duration cannot be represented, it resorts to the production of certain gigantic bodily attributes. Thus the road map no longer serves but to outline (dot-out) a territory, routes, or a scale that doesn't represent this invisible anatomy. And yet, what is hiding the character is what is supposed to be guiding him... Is this reading absurd? Is it called for? Is it interpretive? But it is only the image—moreover, only the isolation of this image.

What has happened? The isolation and the destination of this image—nobody ever dreamed of (or succeeded at) photographing a parent or a friend so maliciously—are a kind of product: there must have been a prequel of movements or actions still perceivable in the image, an entire plot of adventures foreseeable here for us to perceive it as that momentary isolation and suspension of signification where our reading can prowl and spin in the composition of these essential elements. All of the lost meaning and motor force of the film leaves us only with (and already grants us) the possibility of contemplating *destiny*. The latter is not narrative, and we are just barely able to suspect what it was so; it is physical. What has happened? It remains for us as this character temporarily endowed with the weight and surface of paper. We are thus assured that it is readable, that it is hidden, that nothing is written on it, that it is thus indecipherable. It is, even before that, the certainty that it is a game, that the paper's heft isn't destined to endure, but that only we can read the map that sticks to it like an insect. A character has been swallowed up by this planisphere, and America vaguely displays the genitals of this body stuck to some flypaper.

Nana

Something has gotten lost in the image—more than the dry outlines (the style) of the drawing that one can't find in the photographed dress, or the folds that establish the presence of the body upon which the fabric rests.

This transformation, nevertheless, is slower than another subsidence: the white face-cream, its shoddy blandness, and the black around the eyes. The costumer, the tailor, and the fitter always forget that a face not only has a bearing and style that is difficult to dress, but that it has above all, and here solely, a weight. In these silhouettes, the weight of the body is but that of the face, because this one (modified by the stupor and the grimaces of silent film—in expressive films the face does the same work as the entire body in burlesque) is a tragic fall [*descente*], somewhat as one speaks of "a prolapsed [*descente*] organ."

This greasy flour—kneaded, white, and shining—creates a face in an abject state. It seems almost as if the expression has the same force as a rancid odor and ultimately that a kind of fragrance of grease and cruelty inhabits this body that nothing can cleanse of the fat of perverse profit. The lost

elegance of Autant-Lara's extraordinary drawing[12] is that of a modern shrine, or of the same dress weighed down with the jewels of a black virgin. Renoir's photograph, by transforming the gouache planes into cliffs of taffeta and silk, accentuates only the grease of the character—in sum it shows only a face: the beast that has already eaten, and the fat of wrested fortunes dwells here in a black eye and a pout. The vulgarity and extreme brutality of the character are nothing but a universal ravenousness. This being isn't desirable (it is even masked by the hatred of desire); it is simply never sated and can transform the whole world into food.

This food is money, pure and simple; think here of the "chocolate of the Jesuits" in Saint-Simon (the crates off-loaded from a ship, addressed to the general of the Jesuits, containing large ingots of gold each disguised in a layer of chocolate).[13]

This is however a prodigious face: it was a star that got into the habit of making faces and that begins to feel—as if this face felt its origin, because in its very ugliness, at the apex of its social climbing, only power remains desirable and this desire does not make for the trappings of beauty. It is simply this irreproachable mirror in the love of truth, and even the mirror of truth itself—a gaze of white butter. The character next to her in the morning coat would only be a copy; he watches over the spider.

A kind of white butter deposits its cream on the face that continues to darken (to rot and to watch) beneath that same layer. (A whim must have smeared a few expressive lines on the denuded face.) The hardness, the pitiless being of Nana is a photographic phenomenon. In its costume, made for a role (for a "mask"), it pertains to the drawing—in such a way that the missing being or body *here* will have to be deciphered *there*, apart.

The Smoke

The bulge and the athletes (crouching down like women urinating): there is something dramatic in this interlude, in this effect. Beyond even this distribution of roles (the peasants, the general), beyond this loathsome miming, there is the horror (the smarminess) of a social truth that resolves itself in this plenitude and impasse: the truth of gestures, which is to say their reproducibility, is conducive of social essences.

This must therefore be seen as a burlesque theater (and this body is burlesque), to make the Marx Brothers act—that is, to spice up the space with added gestures, true and only far-fetched because, strictly speaking, they are impossible to add to any behavior.

I must not minimize Eisenstein's genius: here we have the horror of the secular and militant sermon, the false general-prince and the true thieves with shaved heads. There is a Jesuit odor that stinks up this sickening smoke.

Shadows

The shadows do not participate in events. They're an architecture that appends itself to characters, a supplement to what furnishes space (stairs, mirror, stool, or wall) in the midst of which, with the additional feeling of these shadows, the actors have to act. The shadow is not an effect of light, nor is it a troubling double; it's—as in theater—a true inner *bearing* of each scene.

A profile, for example, is accentuated or thickened by the projection of another body: the passing of other men erases those who live here, or makes them act twice—the first time as objects (and at the very interior of objects).

And if they begin to consume this shadow? Something else adds itself—for example to Emil Jannings,[14] to his false collar. It's not a variation of light; this supplement is differently perceptible: the actor is endowed with a body or a face of stone.

In Front of the House

Why would a relation exist between uneaten bread at all ages of man, and the shadows that cling to him, detach themselves, and extend unexpected parts of his figure? Nonetheless, there is a silent action of adherence of such shadows on a kind of partition of the world on which bodies (men's, women's, and poor children's) don't remain stuck; and this culminates in the shadow of a man's hat that duplicates (already covers or captures) that of a woman's face. What happens if this woman, relieved of this weight of graphite while losing her light, lightens up extraordinarily and is relieved of the inevitability of eating black bread?

Because, fundamentally, these soot stains that detach from characters like their surface continue the confession of their ancient hunger before our eyes.

The Room

Everyone's gestures have been suspended as if by stupefaction (something momentous has just occurred in the scene); but perhaps because the wheel of the world has turned by an imperceptible notch, because various objects have just changed places, and thus gestures can no longer reach them: they rest in the void, exactly in the emptiness of time.

If the lighting (the light) shifts, the shadows move more quickly than the characters (thereby creating their own sort of reverse-shots).

This is also the dramatic engine of the film: the actors aren't as quick as the objects are in their revolving animation, they aren't as quick as the shifts in lighting, and the fatality is that the lighting alters the profiles and dimensions of a finite number of objects. That in a closed world the journey of shadows is an endless event.

How can one imagine this tableau animating itself or the characters possessing any reality other than that of the photographic portrait if this is the only view one has of the whole space?

It's suddenly like that last chamber one posits behind every novel, where the characters no longer act and can only become written: the closed, inescapable space of insomnia in which these waxworks are perpetuated.

As if it were necessary that these images be—like paintings—endowed with the appearance of an interior life in order for us to see them. I have no need of such an appearance in order to believe in the reality of cinematic images. Indeed, I don't believe in their reality, but rather in that appearance of interior life.

The Carriage, the Veins

The inversion of black and white, of silhouette and background, of shade and illumination, makes the forms, the figures, the coach, and the horses appear like light reliefs on a block of shadow, or like the delicately salient x-rayed veins of a plant of uncertain contours.

It's as if, through this inversion of the positive image, all contours soften, and any body (that is, any object of a gaze) is suddenly conjoined within this mass of ink and bronze that becomes its center, pressing on our perception the notion that the boundedness of a being is not determined by its body or its movements, but can only be read in the *dynamics of its nervature*. Form seems but the illumination and the softening, up to its contours, of these skeletal compositions.

Or is it because the image of this diabolical carriage, swept along on its mad journey, inverted its perceptible quantities—or that, swept along before our eyes by the feverish galloping of bony horses, only this single skeleton of coach, coachman, hooves, and bones could travel alone as if seen from another side of the world, having passed the evanescent, indiscernible frontier of nature's own hell. Not that the speed would completely have swept away the terrain, and that, as a result, a blind world could have moved jerkily along.

The Criminal Life
(The Film)

THE CRIMINAL LIFE

Cinema, even *silent* cinema, has never been able to be a silent cinema: it's more comprehensively a cinema of whispers (subtitles, for example, read softly to children during screenings). And by this whispered silence of first images, the dust, the light, and these gray bodies are returned to us—as if a child, seated within us, still held our hand.

At the heart of cinema (in its most ancient condition for us, and most brutal) subsists the vague terror or fear that links our entire childhood to one film or another. When it comes down to it, why did every film repeat the war? I saw my first films after I'd been immersed in war scenes (air-raid shelters at night, air-raids, exodus, kneeling prayers in a darkened room with bombs going off, dusty cafe and prisoners parading past the windows, nighttime winter travel alone by truck, four years...). But these were only scenes, and scenes that punctured a kind of childhood unconscious. That of a distracted child for whom a voice persisted in the midst of exodus, a tone of voice, music, paintings, objects that the bomb blasts smashed, one after the other, a restrained "air," an existence that catastrophes and bereavements could not bring down; the well, the chasm, or what in any case had no other side.... I

suppose that during these awful times of bereavements, interrupted stays, and chance encampments, a voice, a reserve, and
a sovereign knowledge of being civilized were not destroyed:
the earth did not open up beneath the feet of a distracted
child: no cries were ever emitted near him. And so the music
was sustained, in the night, in the dim light, above the air raid
sirens. Because of what was still the great youthfulness of the
world. Catastrophe couldn't take a step, even through the rub-
ble, even through bereavement, until the day the child was
taken to the cinema. *Shoeshine*: the fear of the war and its four
years of terror, of shattered objects and vanished faces became
fixed in an instant in that particular movie theater, on the
image of that first film.[15] Here began the first sickness he was
guilty of, and for which he'd be punished. The first nervous
disorder—that is, the first uncertain, criminal identity that a
child encountered in fear (in his first true solitude): the ragged
child in Italy shining the shoes of American soldiers. So did
the world begin, that is, become indescribable.

This was how the fear of the war spooked so many children after the Liberation; they became aware of the fear of
having escaped a massacre, but also gained the intermittent
awareness of having nonetheless been dead, because those
films began without that same voice that the planes could
never mask, began without a sister, without help, and with no
smell. Thus began an aphasia, a vanished family, and the
awareness of a crime that preceded all crime. Or that the chat-
tering of teeth was only for Chaplin, Laurel and Hardy, and
Walt Disney. Only in this way did the war never end. *Boys'*

School,[16] for example, made the child's father die, and destroyed a house; Pinocchio[17] killed and deported a few friends. *Skylark*[18] or some screening of Abbot and Costello left nothing but a dining room suspended among the ruins, a wooden horse in a livestock wagon, and a Red Cross convoy and chocolate cups in a Dutch train station.

Fatty's fear, as well as Charlie's and Al St. John's thus began to unhook the entire world from music, voices, and paintings, in a way that was beyond repair. So it was at the cinema that the world began, like the memory of a crime committed against nobody and *forever suspended*. So it was at the cinema that the constancy of a voice, of a *held breath*, heard despite the thunder and so many years, could die for the first time.

Films thus constituted a particular fear, linked not only to a universe of whispers (not a religious whisper and thus something heaven couldn't hear, like hushed words in a room), but also, conversely, to the silence of gray bodies of thin, gesticulating granite.

But there is something more, common to all cinema in a "burlesque" persistence—that is, in the pure invention of movement associated with whitened faces:

There's a shadow, as if the child's father, for example, dead as a result of the war and—because the father's remains, his body, had never been revealed to the child—had been angelically abducted by some force or being toward an unknown redemption, or more certainly toward the effect of an abandonment that instituted the delay of the crime in the comic doubling of the world that he had to go "fish for" at the cinema. And as if this other side of the world—the cohort of angels, the funeral ceremony, the mourners—could only come from there. And that it could only arrive incessantly, in such dejection, by these grotesque rites and, moreover, through this temporary world of fissureless granite where the succession of images or shots and where the reason for all behavior remained a disquieting enigma, that is, exhibited a familiarity and a connivance singularly displaced.

But this is it: the grotesque world attains, as its reason and enigma, such a clumsiness because in a hidden scene of his childhood his father was one day taken from the world as the very reason for the war. And in the midst of bombed villages and crumbling bridges there remained a supreme portrait, a photographed gaze. And if there remained these beings of gesticulating stone in a hasty despair, was it not that all the great men, or rather an entire face of the world, had already ceased—not to live, but to be here and to be able to return, that is, to *come home* and hold out their hands?

But what crime? An objectless distress that fixed itself there uncertainly, or could subsist through the very gap and the difference upon which it was fixed, on anything whatsoever.

Or, rather, if this grotesque world, tilting and teetering, came unhooked and could only repeat a series of catastrophes (that was its engine, simply the reverse of reason), was it not that the day-to-day world could be undermined by an anxiety or a kind of laughter that had already outlasted all the images. Or that allowed no image to persist....

Little by little, a quantity and a force of affects become linked to unknown objects. They immediately have the power to be unrepeatable, indivisible, and unrenewable: unexportable. Thus they don't situate their subject (the site of their constant or consistently likely imputation) in the world—that is, in the milieu where a series of events takes place that can be isolated, detached from all causality, or unobserved... Thus the world, too, is held in the freedom of insignificance; this is why it is, in any condition, livable, bearable, or *detached*.

The unknown affects (born or sought out in a simulator) are of a world that is first of all without an exterior: a world which is defined by a constancy of signification and which only becomes "consistent" by means of these affects, which all have a duration—an internal tension—on their monstrous quantities, that also marks the place of their termination, their annulment (the annulment of their virtual character) or the temporal contradiction at the heart of which this apparently floating world—this granite and flocks of images—is supported by the subject it presupposes. Or that spectator who refilms that entire world and in whom a world of granite moves without memory, or is seized by sentiments *only because of the enigmas of which he becomes responsible*, because that spectator is always here the guarantor or the creator of their reality.

And so it is, more than a complex machine, what it disperses that sees the whole film: the isolated, solitary, or silent instance of the return of a worldly morality that enigmatically flows through these quantities in a weave at once closed (like script and image) but also fully intended, that is, *destined* and addressed to the reality of affects which is the entire expectation or awaiting of the image. That is, destined to crime itself.

The monsters of cinema are, for example, the interior being of cinema: fundamentally, like any of its fictions, beings delegated as anamorphoses of this world predestined to morality—that is, to the signification incessantly addressed to an unknown moral subject, to the one who doesn't synthesize it but in whom strangeness must live like morality—or rather, *last* without being affected by time or by memory.

But who might thus come, having been lifted and perhaps thrown to the heavens in the past—not to fall like all those bombs, or like the descent of a body suddenly slowed down by the opening of a parachute, or a balancing in mid-air—emerging from a quantity of images, out of whiteness itself, to touch, extend their hands, and say "come!"?

And yet the following subsists: the unknown species in whoever watches the film, in whoever sees himself in the film as a new species, that whoever, that opening, those frozen entrails or their laugh make the war begin again. In other words, the cancellation of a being as the reason for the up-ending of the earth. In other words, the cancellation of humanity in ourselves, and of which no representative subsists in front of the *white image*. As if this mosaic face—made of flakes, dots, and dust—simply and without any possible correction, invaded the one who sits before it with the immense extension of a being with no present yet who is bound simply to the mystery of Time, to the horror of Time.

Something, first of all, is linked to the mystery of meaning that we add to the image in our uncertainty of grasping its totality, as we doubt that such an addition would be anything other than an incomplete sampling of what pleas for signification it contains—being uncertain, moreover, that what we add isn't primarily something that we should call ourselves. Beyond the seduction of images, the film will thus keep the mystery complete (and will keep it like a part of ourselves): before any apprehension of new meaning we learn that signification is, here, a body.

This body can't be synthesized. It's not the sum of those parts that we label gesture, grimace, an accent, *some* face and at the same time it's the flight of all this, its shifting perspective, a new amputation of this indisputable set. Such a body nevertheless, and strangely, is first of all (or in a simultaneity of which we had no idea until now, until the world we enter not arrives, borne by this magic lantern) a signification before being the reflection of an anatomy. These two things strike us: there is—and I don't know in what time—meaning without signification, that is, without an operation of parts; that which is projected and animated is not ourselves, and yet we recognize ourselves in it (as if a strange desire for the extension of the human body as signification could act here, or begin to extinguish itself on simulations of objects felt to be a supreme simulation of ourselves: that which isn't born in us may live here). Finally, for the first time, we see humans without shame; that is, humans who, for the first time, are the spectacle of our complete shamelessness. It is thus for the first time a species devoted to possible, unlimited, and infinitely repeatable spectacle that draws us in (that even becomes our inextinguishable need and thirst). And thus, for the first time, and for a final instant, we see what's left of the vanished world: we see complete humans and yet remain entirely innocent of the spectacle.

These humans are infinite. They're constrained by the destiny that represents a history they can never transcend; they are likewise repeatable and may not easily inhabit this universe except through mobile objects—as if their light could define us and as if, within us, in a new consciousness, their scale and proportion could vary even as a dimension of our invisible world. These humans are here through our stubbornness, to repeat that which attaches us to all others in an improbable way, and of which we test the phantasmal bond here: "I would never have imagined that a meaning was an entire body; that is, the sudden disappearance of what attaches me to it."

But why are such words as "guilty," "criminal," or "fault" still attached to this spectacle? The crime is not the act of perpetrating abuses in the world. It designates someone linked by signs to the limits of the universe; and that culprit, before even violating some condition, is such only because the consciousness of this world without freedom passes in him, this world *where he is a link.*

And yet this world has already been seen, and perhaps captured by what we imagine after the fact to be a body infinitely larger than our own (not only because the eye that momentarily projects images of it is a beacon): a larger body, situated invariably behind our own, and behind our head—there, where a sheet of photosensitive cells, such as those of prehistoric animals, is encased in bone. So it is—I can only just imagine—by the leaning of this tilting giant on a white canvas that we see microscopic beings crawl, even though their dimensions surpass those of our bodies. And so we cannot reach the anatomy of this giant being, we cannot inhabit its body as our own.

Yet this is what it is to be at the cinema: perhaps less to forget a body in whose images we are no longer moving—as if its own weight disappeared as its own unfixable images pulled away. We're caught between this giant we must sometimes imagine or assume and what his eye never ceases to film from behind; the first human (the first meaning: it would be an illusion to separate them—meaning cannot be classified— it belongs to bodily states that are successive, conjoined, and unfinished) is inchoate only to the extent that the world does not take place within it. Against its will, that human becomes the transition of a set of forms and meanings that it didn't dream up, and the body that moves on the screen remains the requisite passage of the only world from which it can never be turned away.

I don't believe we're seated in Plato's cave. We are, for an inconceivable eternity, suspended between a giant body and the object of its gaze. So I am not seated, but suspended beneath a shaft of light. That shaft is animated. The slight anteriority of its movement in regards to the animation of the film's objects is visible like a scissor-effect, or as if these rays were kicking their legs, crossing and uncrossing them at irregular intervals.

I don't know how Kafka arrives at this notation, on January 9, 1920, nor what incomplete machine—essentially incomplete yet all the more active at filling in that portion of the visible of which it had been deprived—could end up describing that impalpable relation to the world and that strange accomplishment of the visible world whose perception is nevertheless forbidden to it, and for which it never ceases to be the open wound or blind spot: "A segment has been cut out of the back of his head. The sun, and the whole world with it, peep in. It makes him nervous, it distracts him from his work, and moreover it irritates him that just he should be the one to be disbarred from the spectacle."[19]

Nor do I know, in this confrontation between gaze and body that is a spectacle, how the one watching sees each body that it is separating from act, retreat, and disappear—each body that is henceforth only destined for action and yet that leaves, in its spectator, not so much its image as its former center of gravity, which its immobility preceding action and its solitude before all confrontation required. By means of this lost center of gravity, this body acting so far from us, this same being driven by light, leaves, in those who watch, the nostalgia for its past existence. It doesn't leave its image; it allows that vague point to float or sprout within us, that point which enables it to resemble a silent man, an immobile man. And thus it infects us with all of its sleep, which has passed into us.

"Cinema adds to objects the disquiet of its movement..." Is that how it invents movement? These men, women, beasts, or monsters walk in vain on the canvas of the screen. They don't exactly compose those movements that repeat us and whose nature we can imitate—that is, essential weightlessness. In the same manner as the great scenes, filmed in large cities around the world near 1914, explained the strangeness of the consecutive positions of pedestrians—and how recomposed movement, those slow-motion views of image bodies, and the strange ordered agitation of phantom limbs helped construct artificial limbs for the badly wounded amputees of World War I—these bodies can thus have no sensations as long as they are whole. Sensations, agonies, and fears are like desires composed by a parceling up of the world; at the cinema, we experiment with a kind of "indifference" of the material of the close-up. That operation is not a selection of details; it makes fragments of humans belong to the world of objects, and it is foremost the world of objects, caught in detail, that must generate emotions. That world, subject to complex perceptions, is thus never grasped purely in contemplation. These affects, born of novel and incessant disproportionalities in the world's image, must thus be the medium (*le support*) of the invention of cinematographic movement.

In this way, some of Faulkner's novels invented the cinema—not movement, but a sort of mobility of the frame that ruptures narrative duration or defines characters through mobile frames. We can't see everything there because the imaginary world is the one that least allows images to *rest*, and because these images are taken not for their articulation but for their definition in a series of ruptures. Such images simply reveal that they proceed from a world that is not, foremost, visible. Such images do not add to any past or possible perception; they replace it—that is, they begin to substitute for the world this improbable testimony of an invisible world.

Is it in the same way, in Mizoguchi's *Ugetsu Monogatari*,[20] that the tattooed body of Genjuro the potter is thrown before our eyes? It is surprising, but at the same time no longer surprises us. *We'd been expecting it for a long time*, not as an effect or an image, but as a truth. Perhaps we had been expecting to see here our own body thrown to the earth, our own impossible body covered with ideograms, and having become, for us (for me) wholly written, anatomically indefinite, offered up to its own dermal reading and to its own closed eyes, supremely indecipherable: thus destined to another hell and causing every other phantom of desire to retreat across this burn of ink.

The body, the animal, and the being acting on screen leave us something in their flight. What falls towards us is a probability that is already behind us. This being of images is attached to us, not by a resemblance, but by a center of gravity we would share, whose motion—according to movements accomplished before our eyes—would have the power to transform itself into a shifting (*déplacement*) of feelings, or, more indefinitely, of affects that the images take from us, like a pound of flesh.

In Mizoguchi's film, what we witness through the starkness of costumes and the naked scene, a wounding of signs that consigns the desire attached to the flesh to hell —does all of this show us something that we would know through ancient knowledge, through knowledge linked to time and whose images we have not retained?

Does the same relation inhere with that enigmatic disappearance, that white erasure of a primary body that Kafka evokes? And does something get accomplished in that way: "Like everyone, I too have my center of gravity inside me from birth, and this not even the most foolish education could displace. This good center of gravity I still have, but to a certain extent I no longer have the corresponding body. And a center of gravity that has no work to do becomes lead, and sticks in the body like a musket ball."[21]

Are we seeking a second center of gravity in film (as if it emanated from ourselves) that we immediately cannot locate, because of the illusion attached to bodies, movements, and adventures that endow it with a strange flesh?

But can this be? A center of gravity of the vanished body lives on alone. This center falters towards a more inhabitable world, and does not even require a murder to bring us out of our universe—as if, with that first body, a world had disappeared by itself and the one that remains, lives on, builds itself, and "hesitates" in its appearances were nothing but a hesitation of a world. As if it directed itself or were mysteriously guided, both toward its end and toward an incessant signification of which it would not be the center but one essential part.

Or does this growing imbalance attest to the desire for another world that images cannot construct or simulate for long. In these perceptions or experimental affects that we are submerged in with film, even up to this other form of life made of an absolute modification of perceptible quantities (and even up to these temporalities of action reduced to temporalities of perception), the progressive development of a blurry zone made of the strangest opacity would irremediably hide the unknown matter making up the other world of desire and the second body in the ignorance of which we live. Is it merely an accident that we cannot achieve both except in the dark, and that, moreover, the film leaves embedded in them and floating above us the visible matter of that very night?

The cinema of the spectator also composes this experimental chamber (it's a chamber floating somewhere beyond the world, and in an artificial night); it is experimental only because no solitude, that is, no proper time that thinks the world, increases there. This chamber does not inhabit us—it is rather the space where an *impossible flight is maintained*— because the site of our distress is that space without limits where no image dwells in any deep way, and where none has the power to affix itself.

And does everything reduce itself to this? Seated in the experimental darkness, I enjoy neither innocence nor an immeasurable crime, but I reach without delay (that is, sometimes without conscience) the disproportion of the world. This disproportion comes without a dream—without the derangement or the new combination of any matter in myself—it is immediately a pure affect and, paradoxically, an affect never to be guaranteed permanence by any representation.

Is it because of this that the spectator (sustained by the hope of an unknown body made of antennae of emotions or feelings) would be some part of this turning machine, thrown into what has already been recorded? The spectator seeks this point of gravity (this center) lost only because the body that accompanied it has vanished, or, as if it had been stellified, no longer weighs anything, but is not quite returned to shadow. And the uncertain body, released from this center, relieved of this lead bullet, isn't tattooed or intaglioed by these ideograms that remand to hell (like the princess Wakasa in *Ugetsu Monogatari*) those who decipher in them the letter of their desire; it is only taken up by this disequilibrium, this oscillation, and this incessant fainting. In this way, it is nowhere—its center of gravity is locked outside of itself, floating before all things like a point of light.

For the one who writes, cinema is also very much like a mental universe, not only due to the quality of the images unmoored from the power of resemblance, but also because of their type of solitude, which only produces interruptions between shots within a narrative. This universe is without continuity; something in it—even inside what is simulated—is always ruptured: the catastrophe or the greatest mutilation has already taken place. This anteriority of the drama it does not express is thus like the opening of an interior world. Or does this imperfect recomposition of the world, after its dissolution, still correspond to these physics: "The world has originated from a *general* atom and a single general oscillation—Large and small atoms—Large and small vibrations etc."[22]

And can it be that both the vanished body of which simply a point remains, and the point that seems to attach it to the ground of the image and that would make it fall, coincide, through this apex of unreality, with the virtual point of the image?

Is cinema or film this strange gateway leading—more than to a duration of narratives exposed outside ourselves—to the deepest involution of an interior life and a single interior image? Is this what the state of film should touch within us, rather than the permanence and the truth of feelings that we address as responses to the exterior world?

Writing on cinema might be nothing more here than moving deeper into this darkness lit up by variable points, and reaching the moment where that night appears in us.

But we only see this world through layers of fog, although it is not the same fog that composes the milieu, the aquarium of sorts of our memory. And so, upon leaving the cinema screening, we re-encounter our knowledge (mostly trying to capture it through irony, logical reasoning, attempts to disentangle incomprehensible storylines). After all, what are those screenings but durations during which we are irradiated by an indifferentiated being (indifferenciated as to its knowledge, its memories, its class, and its language) that is probably deposited in us, obstinately amputated of all of its organs yet subsisting there since it endlessly initiates movements, and comments upon our passions by those initiations of gestures that lull us to sleep. As our mass settles into slumber, it is as if that being of desire slowly and violently detached itself, that creature of objects that can touch images and acquiesce to their reality even as we are struck by their implausibility, and even if streaks, jerky movements, and "snow" endlessly corrupt them and even if all color becomes a yellow light. And does that being, that human without birth, constantly require the imperfection of the image, or those snowflakes riddling either a face, a hand, or a wall with layers of soot to reclaim its existence or to touch, through the simple initiation of a moment or of the stirring of desire, the matter that might compose it (but that inchoate being can not last either, since the brevity of every image, and the very disappearance of film make it disappear)?

And yet, in this paradoxical addition of a being to our being, in the sudden rise in us of a ghostly existence, of an unexpected vampire or of a creature who can do nothing but give out long, muffled, or impossible groans that cannot entirely come out through our mouths, it is as if a transparent sleeper were leaning in upon our dreams, and as if, in our center—but this is at the same time behind my eyes, in my chest or in my stomach—a giant aquarium were swimming, equipped like a machine with partitions, breaches, filters of light, and that, in its dimmed liquid, an animal or human without contours were reaching out its hands, or laughing like a dwarf towards all those images whose light it knows itself to be. There is thus that thing, moaning, laughing and swimming, that does not reach childhood, I mean, that can never begin us again—but it is also, deafly, what leads us to those images that we cannot penetrate. Because only that diver lives in them, and moves through them with an agility and a lead that only our feelings can estimate (you are only moved because the fall of bodies in these images has already occurred, through an insensible discrepancy and a faultless eternity, through the temporality of suspended breath, like your body); because, in the end, our skin cannot turn itself inside out completely, through the most extreme tension, to let us dive, bob down and float in that same basin.

And yet this doesn't wake the little human who acted, with its mute mouth, its giant eye and its nimble hands endowed with the promptitude of desires and the very speed of light, or that sketch that was completed in an invisible body that turns its back to any horizon of destiny as Cartesian man, and because that human could exist in a certain place of the world only because a doll, one imperceptibly older or more transparent to time, was urgently shuttered within, yet tied behind its back and slipping into its head without ever residing in a single spot, that is, without infecting its third soul with the slightest stain. Yet, if any initiation of movement in the fatality of enlarged, extenuated and mobile objects, still fatal through the action of an invisible machine more impregnable than those very images, that is to say, through the action of a constant cause whose body we do not discover since it could only be another diamond image or a long thread of saliva shuttered into the surface of the screen, yet if any preliminary jerk or shock that could trigger a movement, a body, an object and a sound stirs that diver, we only ever feel, not the effect of an increase of existence, but that of a mysterious suppression that leaves us, in that instant, seated in that first eternal night—since that being dancing in us, and calling, remains beyond our hands' reach.

So a machine must immediately rotate inside of us (but does it cancel all of our memory as if through the development of its own time, since, despite our claims, we have no memories, that is to say, we possess no images that are simultaneous to those we watch). But it must rotate with jumps in time, so that we might know, as much as possible without understanding it, the effect of that device (*appareil*) through which something moves nonetheless.

Taken up in the haphazard movement of those wheels, are we more bare, amused, charmed, terrified, and pulled in opposite directions, pulled in that time that consists only of images and whose grain and texture seem to be the revelation of their imperfection, or their being once it has grown visible. We are thus pulled by what in ourselves is not an image but is its eye and its nocturnal persistence, that is to say, its inscience, a completely shuttered knowledge that prolongs us indefinitely.

All that is possible for us must end here, as must the imagination of movement through which we continually subsist, so that something of ourselves might be able to detach within this body, a body so close to pouncing and yet which does not reach the horizon of the image, or that hand palpitating in the light, those faces covered in an odorless sweat, or that forest filled with music because they continually disappear, as if they could only disappear within a horizon that remains out of reach of our movements. And consequently, it is as if our criminal existence and our vampire being occupy the entire place and body of our pleasure (*jouissance*) here, that is to say, strictly, its syncopation.

What I am trying to unravel in the enormous massive effect of the cinematograph are not subtle effects (they *exist in a loop*, and never completely or definitely exit a zone of capture in the midst of which I stand as well). Spectators are not exactly the privileged addressees of the effects of cinema—no film chooses them in the way a book might choose its readers to give life to thoughts via a specific precarity so as to constitute their outside, to shelter their world, or to measure their time. Spectators are taken up in that new freedom to watch something of themselves that has never taken place: this paradoxically teaches them their memory.

A new world can live within me and, there, defy time: I do not know what I'll keep most abidingly of it. It must nonetheless disappear in me, and what I'll keep of it is not always the most understandable, nor is it the most enigmatic—perhaps it is the moment of disappearance of *what I was going to understand.*

The destiny of those images is to constitute a memory (and consequently to annex something of myself, and not to become my objects).

Most striking is not the general mobility of the world, but the disquiet added to this movement: I still don't know where these objects move, or whether it is not first within myself that they do so; I am therefore not quite a spectator, but the knowledge of their preliminary death (is this what leads me to the cinema, the deeper reason that brings me there?). The filmed image—in opposition to all other representation, painting for example—has a technical definition that is sensible via its perception; it has no fixed support: I see it because something (a screen cutting through a ray of light) hinders its disappearance; yet it is not completely on the filmstrip, or definitely on the screen, or really in the rays projected by the bulb: I provide the assurance of a transition of the images, so I must therefore be something else than their spectator; I weaken in them.

What, then, is the effect of that perpetual night where I watch (where the progression of images keeps my eyes open)? In that night, I lose the imaginary sphere of movements whose center I was assured to be, and which alone enabled me to act (to walk, to suffer) in the world. I go to that night to lose the world itself, along with this center that I am—for the world is perhaps nothing but the safeguarding of my imagination, and that network where all action (primarily linked and as if anticipated through the imagination of movements) emerges in a sphere of actions and perceptions through which the world appears with myself necessarily as its center, the conscience or the blind spot of those movements that run through it.

In the procession of images on screen, a hand rises, a rowboat sways on the waves, a rotating pane of glass shifts a landscape. All of this lifts us up (lifts a mysterious point of gravity because that very point urgently replaces the totality of our body). It unhooks the experience of finding something sublime from us, something that, if we were to experience it—if we were to go back to being the blind subject of our experiences—would only provoke queasiness or nausea. Any "movement" thus understood, and even the most minimal, up to the object in which it is resolved (a cigarette smoking in an ashtray), is thus liable to attach itself to and provoke that experiment.[23] That singularity of bringing into being, or accompanying, affects that up to then were always born differently, on other objects, on an entirely other terrain, that is to say, affects that were the inaugural traces of an entirely other world. Doubt is never placed on ourselves, but rather on the definition, the extension, the depths, and the very horizon of the world in which we live. Because we cannot transform this world by miming incomplete (induced or inchoate) actions, we doubt all meaning that does not dwell within it. Spectators are simply this: custodians of a doubt concerning meaning. This is the case since their experimental knowledge enables the duration of what follows (and the spectator's entire cinematographic conscience is nothing but this): that no object, not even the slightest parcel of a universe or the smallest grain of dust, is anterior to the disturbance of meaning that assists its birth and death, as roman goddesses used to do. That disturbance and suspicion, that indecisiveness of meaning at times, are the only immobile part, and the only silence, in the uninterrupted course of images. Yet these images, before being animated, are simply images, yet images that are so specific that ancient painting, for example, does not contain them, which is to say, can no longer "contain" either their definition or their duration.

To try to understand something that I am feeling, I go back to see an action film. The same effects are still produced at the same time; and yet, I've changed (my age, my language, the quality of my emotions). Does the film have the power to repeat its first spectator (and did something of our life, which we would have never known, grow immobile before those images)? Truth be told, this film will not find spectators who are arranged like machines of nerves and intelligence. Rather, the film will take beginning sketches of reasoning from them, or beginnings of the kind that cannot be continued: in other words, it provokes apocopes of words in them: no one will accompany the film with their voice. Does film thus create a kind of listening body in that night in which we sit?

But then what causes the sublime? And what is that power of sounds, words, and images to displace something unknown in us that we nonetheless recognize—and is it not for that very reason that we recognize it? What is that power to make us acquiesce, for example, to that pain, to the memory of that pain that we'd never suffered as our own?

We undergo here what we might conceive of as anticipations of desire. These murders, these possessions, and all of these prehensions—a hand or a gesture on the screen, for example, once seen, cannot be imitated but is covetable—are defined with a new weight, perhaps a total weightlessness that makes them also disappear. So we don't look at these for long as parts of objects, but as whole bodies that are liable to have been our horizon. Such anticipations of desire don't simply fade out on objects. I can't tell the story of a film, for example, because I can't escape the definition of the image. Nor can I escape the fragmentation of images (of shots, frames, angles) that does not divide its narrative but cuts up its substance beyond movement (the first movement is not that of the characters, but the one through which the camera enters, glides or flees parallel to objects). So it's from very far away that I recompose that story that wasn't represented, by forgetting images or by connecting a few of them. I myself grant some credibility to a narrative that is continuous despite images. It is me again who experiences that kind of novel, the lacunae of which are mostly what I've been granted.

Immersed in that perpetual night, I run the risk of learning nothing of these images, and of representation, since I am there at the finish line as their judge and the instance (that is, the imminent possibility) of their suppression: I am there to add nothing to them, simply so that the rollover of day to night might cease in me for a hundred minutes or so, and so that the virtuality of these objects, emerging in this night where no sleep is possible, can be cancelled in my fear, in the confused and sudden range of my emotions.

We do not experience these desires as the relations between objects and ourselves, but as whole bodies: they are qualities (ways), not anatomies.

The greatest terror, the most contrary feelings (for whom I must be the momentary custodian or the sustainable memory: to say the truth, I don't know what fixed role I'm given here) coexist in this lightness of objects: to lift a world would only require sliding a hand or an index finger among these objects—if I didn't run the danger, on the contrary, that the rays that compose these images might reduce my entire body to dust.

This imaginary world does not affect me; the actions travelling through it do not cross through my life. Yet it is the world I want through these bodies and appearances that sustain my obscure desires. I wait for them to grow immobile without being decomposed. The fatality of this world is maybe simply this: it is decomposed in me, more than I reign over it. It escapes me more or less in its totality.

Is it here, on these bodies, accompanied by the haze of their matter through an uncertain world, that we've learned to play with the life of others for our own pleasure, so as not to trouble our most profound disquiet, and the uncertainty of meanings that our entire life cannot name or usher into the world, and in this way, do we bring that disquiet to life in several worlds at once? Or is this permanent crime, whose power of effigy—rather than its imaginary accomplishment—transfixes us before the film, constantly hidden within us, and does it grow as it imprisons us in its girth?

THE LESSON OF DARKNESS

So we see that dust is only temporarily affected with a body: the dust of light has a greater permanence, dust that is not even breathable and whose bodies go away in the end. Those dancing grains are not made to be seen, they aren't the phenomena, or perhaps they are simply the awaiting of a specter and the strange menace suspended in the memory of children—for we never see light destroy itself in that way, become decomposed, and produce colors in our room as it glides over glass objects. Neither does it replace the scorching wind on the sand.

This smoke does not shelter or hide anything, not even the physical reason behind the fact that there is no body or shred of anything that can last beyond our gaze. This is accompanied by the thunderous rumbling of the actors' voices; it is as if the size of the images and their unboundedness, which no longer corresponds to any scale, as if all of this gigantification enabled us to withstand such amplified sounds—or, as if such enlarged sounds, as if seen through a magnifying glass, were necessary for those huge faces, necessary so that those faces and those giants' kisses did not appear muffled, nor those dwarves' smiles constantly stupid rather than disturbing. In short, it is as if the sum of all that unboundedness reached a proportion isolated beyond the world, one that neither composed a replacement of sorts nor the truncated fiction of fragments blended in with the history of men, but made instead a few giant faces projected in the night of cinema so as to plug all the visible interstices in the street, so that these faces would fill, not only all streets of a city—making the bustling and the hurried footsteps of its inhabitants, reduced to lines of twitchy points, visible on their most illumined parts—but, with faces infinitely the same and almost without magnification, would cover the entire surface of the earth with the same smile, the same wink of an eyelid, the same stubby, ring-laden fingers of a cruel Nero, and could freeze all humanity through the same audible whisper through which would transit, because of an unfinished war, American words and slaves.

This grumbling thunder, these mouths, and these eyelids applied to actions that no whole person could have led, remained for a long time incomprehensible. Before we understood them in their chain of succession and in their causes, their effect made us feel that gods, or some complete hell (even during the lightest comedy) were in vain reaching out to touch us. The effect of images remains below the threshold of their figurative organization (we are constantly forgetting this, as if what struck us firsthand was the technical framing of the image): as soon as the film begins, they initiate the wait for something that will never happen: this is even what guarantees their credibility, their duration, and their memory: that the sum of emotions acting within them (acting at first only in vain, for all they do is transform a story that has little credibility) would end up replacing the world.

But is this also why we go to the movies? So that the first gap (*décalage*) and the first crack in time (in the world and in the history of our memory) would finally be filled and be closed again at the very site where they were opened.

This time which we haven't experienced, or if we've done so, only in images (through the resurgence or permanence of images), blends in with our life—more strongly than any figure from novels we've read—and perhaps as far back as we find the memory of these images to have a greater duration, to be less prone to distortion than our childhood memories, that is, to not be taken up as they are in the uncertainty of our age at the time, in the uncertainty of age, or size, or of the world of adults that still struggles against the edification and permanence of such memories, absent the stability of images or the aspect of those memories for they still now belong to the time that has passed in us—time for which our entire present and our changing body is the most complete forgetting, or which no illness or suffering of time can allow us to recover more completely. If the return of these film images is better and less distorted by our memory, that is to say, by all this time that has been the confusion of my body, it's not that I saw them better (plunged in the night of cinema where the darkness momentarily brought them into relief), but that these images were quickly detached from the films and the suggestions of time that linked them into syntheses that were foreign and as if exterior to their most profound effects—that of being self-evident *and* incomprehensible—and that their power of duration emerged only from the fact that they photographed us in the past, through successions of night, outside of the time we were living—outside of the joys and disasters of which we were not fully conscious. We were photographed by these first images, and only this can explain the vague fear that subsists even in the greatest pleasure that we encounter in them.

But how can we maintain the implausible character or the paradoxical formulation of such certainty, the certainty that these images only remain within us, and come back to us so vividly not because we mastered them in our encounter, but because they photographed us during our childhood and outside of that childhood's unease (that malaise of time and of the whole consciousness of duration that is the substance and suffering of childhood)? It is but the fiction of a mechanical human—who commands the effects of its sensibility as if handling objects, and little by little, who has at its disposal simply a representation of time—it is but the image of that experimental mannequin that turns us into a simple manipulator of indifferenciated images, and produces after the fact (like a necessary excrescence) the absurd equivalence of all objects reducible to visible objects and to the general structure of perception (that is, of final reproduction) of that visible.

We only ever see the part of the world that would make the extension of our virtual body (the anticipation and imagination of our movements) possible. And does this hold together—not to embrace, to synthesize or to append their circles but to give mass to a single sphere—the imaginary forms, colors, and movements that link us precisely to the center of our body.

This is why a landscape, a street, or our bedroom is visible or memorable, because it is populated or infested with a multitude of indeterminate or simply inchoate affects, all of which roam those spaces whose center, whose unknowing (*inscience*), whose entire gaze, and whose mute center we inevitably are, for we do not imagine ourselves simultaneously in two points of space. We are always the most invisible point of crystal.

Thus cinema begins something specific here: it makes that point of gravity disappear (that point through which virtual points exist in our perception independently of all structure or of all specular phenomena: and this simply secures vision through the imagination of movement, not through its possibility—it is the antecedence of a motion without the verification that requires that we *go see*); it thus makes the world disappear in us, erases us from the world in one sweep. Imagine this: it crosses us out for an undecidable length of time, yet a moment that will endlessly play on in our memory (not as duration but as an event that can be reduced to seen images). Such an event is not primarily of a perceptible nature. This is not only because all film images (any image projected in that sunless world) are accompanied by *absolute affects* that play on simulating our body, but also because they are the suppression of our world. This constitutes an enjoyment (*jouissance*), although it is the delayed enjoyment of a moral being; such pleasure is thus always a crime, the crime of an amputation on ourselves, one that links us, at our age and in the middle of our life, to an enjoyment that is so entirely innocent because we can never claim what follows from it as if it were a choice or happenstance, nor use it as the deliberation of our moral being. But this remains within the crime, in a muffled and improbable way, only because I expect these images, these played actions, or these affects granted to something within me to have a real immediate or mechanical development. In short, after the world momentarily became my entire blindness, not only to what remained *outside* during the length of a film, nor to the persistent and unrelenting war occurring in front of the screening room, but also to myself as the indecisive center of incessant travels through the world that I fed daily with my eyes, in short, after or despite all of this, the only expected development to the incredible or entirely banal acts that I'd seen would be an absolute destruction and incessant trembling of the earth.

But it would be a destruction accomplished in such a way that I would hold no responsibility for it—or that its causes would not even pass through me for an instant (nor would they pass through my conscience, my perception or my action, that is, they would have no power to affect my memory). The reason for this, for now and quite as incomprehensibly, is that I can never leave the moral chains that touch the conscience or the imagination of responsibility within me for very long, not only during any new or preexistent war, but even with the slightest geological accident that affects the surface and arrangement of the earth. Because, through the greatest mystery, the fullest and most repentant part of myself is immediately, or already, *over there*. And because, through that same mystery, and even more horribly in all places and in all theaters of human abuses that I hear about, I am already, as if already eternally, the victim, the executioner and the ordeal itself, that is, the elaboration of the crime that I wish to stop. It circles within me I don't know where, and neither behind my eyes nor in my chest can I reach that point that attaches me entirely to the world.

Outside, the world is constantly maintained (and neither does the spectacle grasp it, enclose it, or reflect it). As we exit into the light of day, it's always a surprise that buses circulate, that movements carry on. Only the rain upon leaving the movie theater extends the film a bit—it extends or perpetuates the same kind of continuous hatching through which objects can touch us constantly.

So we saw an earthquake, monsters, or a love story on those giant faces. And we were assured of the essential inexistence of our world. And once again we immediately fell into the impossible and simultaneous sleep of all humanity.

And yet, the buses surprise us by continuing to circulate, or our memory immediately succumbs to this city, because those images we've seen and which cannot last nonetheless underscore something which was certainly not born prior to them; isn't it also like a conscience, lost in the middle of all this, led astray by the noise and movement that has multiplied in space, and that begins again, all of a sudden, in the same way as it had stopped, and also emerges abruptly from the night? Through those other movements, those scales of gestures and giant words, we'd have learned that the destiny of our race and of our species was to be trampled as it had never been by these heroes, heroes who accompany us until death without growing old. And to be still trampled—for heroes have never done anything else—by those beings who do not even have the uncertainty of those characters from novels we've read whose images are barely able to last in us. And they trample our hearts in those dreams we stubbornly refuse to construct.

This world, *already exhausted* although I know not why, does not come toward us or pull us to itself: it changes us momentarily—in order to be seen, it demands that we perceive our own shrinking before it, or more exactly that we perceive this: we do not face it, we are simply that world: we are its reality (*réel*).

Is this why these images trample us if they resemble us? It's not true that they make us think (that's an exception, an acquired effort). It's not true that they are a kind of free imaginary, that is, one acquired without suffering and without any experience of the time that cannot be formulated within me (the time over which I reign but which I cannot keep because the earth will topple over, for example, or the night will spread around us): they *knock us down* because their resemblance to us occurs through another face and a wholly other composition of time on the body.

With my impotence I accompany the terror greater than my body (it experiences me more than I, myself, feel it), the sly pleasure beneath a low ceiling, the warmth of a common indiscretion, and the sublime surges that, just like a clumsy dancer who can only follow with a foot the music that should send him flying across the stage. For all of this I will die so far from images, so far from touching them, so far from their light: I am certainly all of their reality.

Images invariably choose us at the same age. This isn't a real age, or a childhood that was truly lived; it is more certainly a kind of childhood transition that remains immutably attached to the first encounter that occurred in this very spot. And that could teach us something about time, if it were not a disappearance of time that the simultaneity of two worlds in which we are momentarily immersed makes us experience.

We only learn to see a kind of aquarium: or we become conscious that those fish are only there because we put them there, that they are in water, and that this is the torture to which we subject them. That's why they look at us as if they were the full consciousness of that ordeal whose cries we do not hear—consequently, a fish language must exist that remains inaudible to us *because of the time* through which, for example, we are carried far away from that red-dened water.

(Am I also that mechanism through which captured fish exist whom I don't hear because I don't stay long enough or small enough for that, or because of that aquarium glass sepa-rating us with an additional eternity: something of a child must swim here, endlessly skimming the eyes of those crea-tures, mute and full of blame because of that still water...)

These stirrings of movement, measured by certain collapses within me, don't fill me with a nascent will for action, but instead with the full anticipation of the new possibility they announce, that is, with a nascent will for a world. Or perhaps with the desire, not of that body shown over there, and of those undifferentiated bodies, but the deep desire for an unknown planet where a body's weight would exist outside its mass, for example, enabling such blinding acts, the conscious-ness of restless actions, or long lethargies without sleep or without any other consciousness of all that time that makes images grow old in us: those bodies, which we see projected, acting, or caught in the light, do not contain a third image in themselves, *although they resemble us*. Are we the image that they constantly cannot form? In this way, they constitute the most impossible transition of *our knowledge as action*.

But that knowledge is uncertain, and more or less unfor-mulated. That is why it can act over there as if through a delegation of ourselves that we've never wanted, and to which we nonetheless fatally acquiesce.

A river used to be flowing here, on the site of Babylon. I can only guess at it on this dry earth or through these great fish with human faces that emerge and disappear with the blinding flash of lightning.

The stubbornness of phenomena, or, in a sense, the continuation of the overall being of phenomena, despite changes in appearance or in the major aspects of reality, is not what makes us see a lake on this patch of irregularly ridged, grainy asphalt with its calculated lighting. Being in this puddle and this narrow basin shuttered in a film studio is like a lake. It's like being in a cardboard cemetery with leaves raining down upon the tombs, and a fog machine, where an atom of the destiny of the characters develops, moves, or is played out, as through a muff. On these few signs through which we grasp the lake, accept it, or recognize it as a kind of truth with no evidence (it doesn't strike us as a revelation but encounters in us a quick acquiescence that burns those signs we do recognize), it continues or completes itself within us, with the sound of an inaudible lapping, through the dregs of silt, the thick water and the reeds surrounding it: we do not really need its most complete truth, or for this appearance to be verifiable through details; it's like a lake seen through layers of fog, heard through a voice coming from an uncertain distance, the slow rocking of a woman's body rising above the end of a small boat and rowing, the gliding of this boat on some identityless substance—which is the melody lost in space and probably sung somewhere one can hear it from very far away, the fog, the slow movement of the body and the gliding of the boat. It's because this action unfolds or flows without events that it perpetuates its image like a lake.

This sequence from Mizoguchi (*Ugetsu Monogatari*), and this example, which is just one among thousands, does not make us acquiesce to an action and its frame because it confirms some intimate representation we'd have of the silent water, or because it encounters the image of a lake as it would be enclosed in our memory, in travel recollections, in dreams (in truth, such an image would be composed only of thousands of shards of different sizes and forms that could never compose the full shape of a lake we might have seen or which we could synthesize through our knowledge of this possible surface lying somewhere in an unknown corner of the world). It is that event, that apparition without action that remains, reflects itself, and then disappears like a lake, and it is on that boat that those moments and spaces of song, movement, and slow rowing come together and yet also pass because *it was a lake* and, adding itself to all the spaces we've never been for ourselves that song, and that intent sculling in pasty mist, that straggling fog belies the truth of all the places that we have been, and suspends their image for its entire duration. The duration of this scene is thus the synthesis of fog, of voice and silhouette in which no bodily memory of mine has ever had me live, because as I swim and roam through another lake in a motorboat, rowing through a lagoon, I've never completely been there except through more complete awarenesses of cold water, of the sound of the boat, of passengers, of conversations, of the strain and blisters on my hands, of mountains and pine-covered slopes or of houses on a bank to which this effort did not lead, because we were rowing in this thick atmosphere like an immobile swimmer. I wasn't there, except through the consciousness of places that I'd left, hunger perhaps, or the desire to enjoy instants that could not annihilate me—I see that this Japanese boat begins its glide again, brushes past fog and starts to sing although we cannot see the mouth from which this melody comes, and the enchantment and subjection of all the memory that has never transited through my body in such a synthesis, does not begin. What begins is a place of action that can't be copied, an inhabited place, that is, one where there is no possibility for any additional gaze, and yet a place that is entirely virginal within me. That place adds its sublime through an accuracy and disproportion of all gestures, through a quality of night that will never return to the world where I am groping blindingly in a single silhouette that my entire life cannot copy: only this pulls me into a loop, ends its variations, can suspend in me all action in view of that slow passage, my entire life can be strung together through that repetition that I'll never know how to mimic. I'll never perform that rocking of an oar, of a mist. I'll never sing that melody: all of this lasts in me and something must thus have acquiesced to this movement, something must have recognized this place I've never visited, the point of that surface of water where I've never been as if all navigation had stopped before I reached it, and where that now silent song still resides. And in that image which will die because in a moment of action that's become incomprehensible, and in that sequence that suspended my entire memory, that stopped the uncertainty of that body, suffering from immobile actions and endlessly falling back into all the points of its perception in the hopes of finding its mass there, and as if through that incessant groping that maintained it in the world it would no longer experience time, nor the aging of time, because, in a single instant to whose image it could string itself and which would erode, that slow shaft of gray action, its melody and imperfect dusk were a lake.

And yet I am not surprised to recognize those places I've never reached, where nothing of myself has ever been that blinding emotion, or on the contrary, a drowsiness and an incessant bodily duration (for cinema only offers these simulations of action, even those who sleep are active there, because they are images, that is, perceptions caught up in the time of another action that will carry their sleep out of them, and also carry out the memory we will retain of a passing resemblance to sleep). Those novel places, those unheard of songs and voices are not in myself: rather, they incessantly recognize me, and here is where is accomplished that through which we acquiesce to sublimity, through that impossible transition of our knowledge as action that is nonetheless maintained.

But we never (in truth, *ever*) comment upon this as the core of the films we've just seen, or as the least futile reason (since it's not an excuse) we go to the movies. Nor do we say why cinema is, after all, a machine to manipulate souls (and tell what additional reasons we could supply on the dangers or stratagems of using that machine). This is what provides us either with closure or completion, or makes us expand, indifferently. This is what makes something momentarily gravitate into a parenthesis that might just barely compare to a hospital visit, where I can be that perfect subject, at once relieved and terrified, both submissive and docile, to be palpated, examined, irradiated behind cold plates stuck to my stomach, to be told that someone knows what is afflicting me or whether I am healthy, to hear that the beatings of my heart are not my entire life but the impeccable science of a man with small glasses, or of an inelegant nurse with a bad hairstyle, a parenthesis that might just barely compare to those cold hands palpating limbs, or to those instants during which, as I give myself over to a science I expect nothing of, knowing full well that the entire truth of my body is not there, that under those frog-like palpations I don't expect anything, and that, in one go and as one single exception I succeed in thinking of nothing—another man must have arisen before those filmed scenes and consented for me to the entire infidelity of my knowledge, since I've never wanted it to be reduced to actions (and I even constructed my entire life to evade that very thing).

Thus I recognize that precarious place and instant passing on the screen, not because they are guardians of my imaginary (in truth, my imaginary is simply a memory, a perfect repetition of a time that could accomplish itself by keeping all the time that has since been added to it, by keeping an enchantment of twenty years ago intact in today's body). I recognize that precarious place and instant, which suspend my memory and the time that cannot be added up for the body that I suppose has always experienced them, in the entire treachery of my life—my knowledge has thus become a fatal action.

And yet, such knowledge is not what we've added to our-selves. Neither is it that immense event of speech, or that indefinitely written surface lake (*nappe*) that I want to become, and whose awaiting and incessant activity is the most imperious reason of my infidelity to those with whom I live. That knowledge is extreme. It is simply the periphery of the gestures where the being that we are is annulled, beneath our eyes and in our limbs: it is my sleep, it is all of the movements that remain invisible in part, those move-ments through which I smoke a cigarette, eat, do not think of anything, movements through which I am simply without any desire for expression. This (that I've never seen in any spectacle nor in any human creation, whether it be painting, sculpture or theater) has incomprehensibly or suddenly become an action. But this is not where I recognize an action that I've accomplished. And in the regret that my entire body, my age, conscience and landscape did not add up or not reach a synthesis in those fingers resting on a piano or that extraordinary puff of smoke, it is that action that will never weigh in my invisible gestures, because I've missed it— since the totality of the world relies on it, not just a film character's impatience or worry. So it's on this spectacle of stone residing in the infidelity of a single gesture that all of the knowledge through which I am invisibly linked to the repetition of humanity is exhausted.

And so I search in these comedies and tragic gestures, both suffused with the same fatality and infidelity, for that incom-prehensible and incessant repetition through which all our knowledge, because it is blind, becomes an incessant action, an action that is troubling only because it is indefinitely ourselves, ourselves who are here and who do this because we never acquiesce to others' gestures and can't imitate them because their body has a history, and we suspect that through their eyes only the story attached to that body can see us. And so, despite everything, because the newness of our desires is due to the unformulated conviction that our body, and our body alone, has no history, this single infidelity of action of our knowledge is also a constant desire. But right away, any gesture on screen will initiate and realize the exceptional duration and entire life of a monster.

The cry that we were going to emit, and that stays caught in our chest, the cry that we have emitted in such a way that it will stay forever caught in that chest and only linked to that very moment, that very image, that single image moment—do we experience it as soon as our chest heaves and emits an inaudible "Ah!" Do we experience it as soon as the image passes, and that the cry is larger than the image—because it couldn't appear, arise, and answer aloud without destroying the images that follow this one (and the substance of those images which demands our immobility)? By creating an echo that remains mute, does the cry prove, not the grandeur of the scene or the abruptness of these images, but the fact that we have no voice because we are the sublime instance of that entire image (in that instant it becomes larger than the world, and yet we are even larger, and even more so because of that pent-up cry: the cry could have said "yes" and made the image die—but then it would only have killed that unknown pleasure, unknown because it had no body).

Or is it because the unique, jerky movement of a single crowd, of a single movement followed through this multitude of angles, shots, frames or fast-forward effects cannot stop the eruption of Mount Vesuvius, or all the rains of the world, or that it wakes the drowning of Pharaoh and of his army—this disaster guarantees my permanence, it volatilizes the rain or snow that was falling outside, and to say the truth, folds the world like a cage in which only the shadow of a prey roams for an instant.

And yet I play no part (in either intention, deliberation, or memory) in the crime that is committed before my eyes. I am but the site of its revelation and the consciousness of its inevitable nature—that necessity and that knowledge are simultaneous, as linked as the stab of the knife, the hat that falls to the ground, or the upturned eyes—and yet if I can do nothing else but unite the flapping of action to passages of objects and gestures, I am nonetheless the only site where the time of this crime has a duration—that duration is immediately within me; is it not myself? It must be so, because, as its analysis strings itself out on screen, I already feel the relief of that act whose delay I perceive in the images. No one moans better than I do, no one pushes the dagger in with a more pronounced "haw": I feel both the delay of the action on my desire and the relief (the cancellation) of that desire on that action which does not represent it. That crime is not in my desire, it doesn't constitute its entirety, nor does it represent it, and yet it stands in for it. And in that very failure, doesn't it fulfill that indecisive part of my desires that is always without an object. It's a will, but as soon as it takes on the character of an action it resolves the error of a desire wanting to affect the face of the world, that is, wanting to remove something and, if possible, to be the consciousness of what I am removing.

And yet, *that crime which was not in my desire wasn't either its entirety.* It doesn't magically relieve the responsibility I'd never have taken since I have no memory of its cause. In me, it accomplishes a movement of sleep by relieving the delay of a world that is without a figure, form, or name: it will always and eternally be delayed in relation to the shadow of that prey that roams within me with no destiny, and which I cannot confess to for it has no truth.

Neither the hat that falls, the hand that strikes, or the manhunt can expand or lessen the ghost of the crime that I do not commit: before that image, I am implacably the more sovereign knowledge and the eternal consciousness of a more accomplished, more universal infamy because that preemption of any act within myself has no object. Thus, in the midst of represented actions, I can constantly change the proportion of those acts through the measure of the world, and thus, most of all, constantly change the measure of the world. But I don't maintain any freedom in the actions whose parts, or frag-ments, I see modulating within me and becoming my momentary meaning; there is no relief of that part of judg-ment or irony maintained outside of them; I become fatality here: I am thus strictly that world and *the consciousness of its use*; that use only occurs within it, can only last within it: it is the perfection added (but in an inchoate way) to these acts and whose guardian—whose meaning—I am.

I've always been surprised that thinking about film is done in an instrumental way, giving us the function and safeguarded place of manipulators of the image. But we don't have the power to manipulate images; that is, we only have that margin of signification because we are a part of the image. Signification does not involve us here through a sovereign decision that would be our consciousness, or through an impregnable instrument that would be our culture—as if it were an element that had been added to us, one that was certainly real "since" a few of us might precisely be reduced to "that," to that kind of non-completed being. We only manipulate meaning through a part of us that doesn't let anything else subsist. The work of meaning doesn't primarily occur through signs; it is the invention and transition of signs that accomplish us momentarily. And so it is also the work and consciousness of time that doesn't produce a world. This is why that very particular pleasure (*jouissance*) is insistently called suffering—a suffering that is not linked to a particular suspension of the world but that is linked to the fact that this privileged transition of meaning, which I can be, does not last in regards to the time that suspends the world.

Am I destined to feel this transition and this entire absolution of the world, of time, and of other unceasing events, exactly where I did not produce it as *my* cause, *my* oeuvre, or *my* doing? Is this what I feel and expect at the movies; does even the most idiotic film satisfy this expectation? Yet what I experience there is that my knowledge returns to me as a desire for action, that such action is not in my desire, and that such desire, although momentarily satisfied and diverted from its fatal absence of object, was not the entirety of that crime. So I go to the movies to discover that measure which does not link consistently to my pleasure, or to the entire gamut of affects that roam within me. I'll commit that unknown crime and that unheard of pleasure: I can't answer to what meaning I become there; that's why it will revert back to being incomprehensible in my memory, or impossible to formulate. Perhaps this unique desire comes down to this: to be in the image, to be meaning and its privileged transition, and not to understand it, that is, to become powerless to *move back through it*.

So will I learn and take pleasure from time? Something will accomplish itself in us; a sleeping action.

Each image of the film (each shot or each frame) is reflected by a shard of mirror; one single body, for example, could thus be represented according to its parts, each part needing a shard of mirror. All of these images together—images that were each independent originally (legs were moving around, dancing or jumping while the hands were busy, for example, writing, and the mouth speaking, smiling, or chewing)—do not compose a film but a territory made of strips of movement, or of stops of movement without any link; their link can be imagined as a plains—or rather, a clearing—where all of these mirrors are arranged in a circle, in a hemisphere, or in the form of a cupola: all that matters is that they be equidistant from one point in space: there, at that point, at the very center of all the animated images, that is to say, at the same distance from each, is an immobile spectator who can only successively see the movement of the images, via the slightest shift of the head or of the eyes. Despite his position and the circular arrangement of the pieces of mirror, the spectator cannot simultaneously encompass all the reflected movements. His body is immobile, or nearly so, and nonetheless this mosaic vault, each mosaic animated with part of a whole movement, does not represent anything for him: whether this concave hemisphere moves closer or farther from him, that is to say, from the point par excellence, or whether it clings to him tightly, or gives him space to move, it wasn't their unfolding that made his visual sphere tangible, because such images do not reflect back the point from which their reflective surfaces are equidistant. The spectator thus cannot imagine acting while he sees these images, he does not flee his body in his vision, so he isn't remanded to it: not only is that body not the center of that particular visual activity, but furthermore, the point on which that body is situated in space has been calculated so that, none of its perceptions belonging to it, it cannot imagine itself after the fact to be a hub for the appropriation of images, that is to say, to maintain the power to cancel them as if he were producing them. The character situated in such a place is at the exact site of the abandon (*désappropriation*) of his perceptions: he was placed by the manager of the show in the only place in the clearing, or in that plains, in which his body disappears. The arrangement of the fragments of mirror, and not the character of what is reflected in them, is such that this banal spectator can in no way glimpse a reflection of himself: he is thus situated on the site and on the geometric point that render him absolutely invisible.

An indifferent spectator who has become that very point sees his visual and mnemonic capacities increase: series of double punches, in an endless stream, smash against lips from which seep a trickle of dark liquid, an embroidered handkerchief drops like a leaf on a hardwood floor and causes a stiletto to slip, tanks rumble with a great clinking of chains through the center of a heap of smoking ruins, one of the tanks lurches up, reveals its paunch as in a grin, and immediately unveils its human gaze. Rain falls on a group of kids splashing in the puddles looking for a tennis ball, an officer from the Tsar's guard clasps a dairywoman to his dolman in a powerful embrace, a forest flattens under the spread of lava, a bouquet of violets falls very slowly from a box in a theater. The spectator is invisible, he follows the luminous shine of large lips mouthing foreign words and contracting into an expression of disdain, he repeats these words internally without learning that language and forms his mouth into a pout with the conviction that this is the greatest disdain he can express, while the rain is falling, bombs are exploding, forests are catching fire, clumps of mountaineers are tumbling down the slopes and a boat, two boats, like a handful of peanuts, are continuously tossed about on waves that toss them—with reflections that cling to one of their names—against a wall of foam, and then a stronger slap spins them back, one, two, shaking in the middle of the image while their masts swing dangerously. The spectator glimpses, in the backlighting of the images, his hands and the end of his pant legs with shoes. He kisses ten American movie stars, wears ten different mustaches and as many suits, shoots a poisoned arrow into Attila's back, picks up the red phone, leaps between Fabiola and the lion, loses consciousness on the final beach during D-Day. He does not sleep, he does not exhaust any desire, he is completely invisible, more ferocious than all tigers, quicker than lightning; all the images pile up on top of him and disappear; he is immobile, he can only pronounce the most incomprehensible words and forgets them because faces rot once they've enunciated them. All the images fall beside his body but he rots very slowly, before his gray hair Jayne Mansfield's breasts swell beneath a nylon blouse and pop off a button, he moans in silence, the same shoes shift at the bottom of his pants, he grows old very slowly before the ocean. He does not sleep. He grows old before a herd of dinosaurs. He is invisible.

The lingering desire to be in these images the consciousness of what will disappear as if through my action accomplishes within us a sleeping action—but that is a desire to be, if possible, the consciousness of what I am removing in being insistently where I am removing it, because I am insistently the slightly anterior knowledge of the object that will disappear.

While watching Renoir's *La Chienne*, the "bitch" became the object of a murder long before she died. That deferred murder simply made its execution impossible for an instant, and, for that single instant, all of my knowledge was simply the palpitation of that delay which designated my prey while perpetually pulling it out of the field of my action. And yet, once that act was accomplished, once there remained no object of action, it was as if, through a decision born of the movements of my sleep, I had moved abruptly after a long while of suffering the inconvenience of a position without being able to articulate the movements that might have enabled me to turn around; any hand I had not used for deliberation had abruptly shifted me, and the suddenness of my new position was nothing but the time of that uncomfortable immobility. This is how I can explain to myself that Renoir's "bitch" dies too late, that the tangible atmosphere of that crime colors it for so long, enshrouds it, and turns it into that blinding light that we must shut off.

How can we explain that a nonexistent beast was granted space and emptiness, and that such a beast could not become visible but could simply fill that space, advance within it, and that we could only hear its breath? Is that white space, that emptiness, a kind of expectant body embedded in the field of the image?

Once the murder is accomplished enigmatically before my eyes, will I (or is this simply a possibility) learn that it contained a larger amount of data than I had imagined? I can think, and compose in my memory, that I was present to the crime, when all I experienced was the anatomy of the body of slow-motion actions that preceded it, that extended its deliberation between myself and the actors, and that finally spirited away the very scene, as if the censorship of forgetting had befallen it; prior to the unfilmed gestures of the actors, I will have made those fateful actions through their bodies; my decision, strengthened by that slow contradictory and irreversible deliberation, by Legrand's confession of tenderness and destitution—because he is simply looking for an ultimate object, so that the world whose threshold he will cross might only perpetuate the moment of his confession and reproaches, and their common light as they settle on that woman—my decision or my assent in the delay of the action would simply have muddled the image of the murder in my eyes. The latter was simply the musical duration of that scene, which is not reducible to extreme acts. These acts are perpetrated during the only moment of obscurity in that room, and as if through that accident of light, I discover the deed when I reenter through the window (I'd left without having any memory of my flight) and see, in a slight disorder of the bed, a changed position of the two bodies, the sweetness of the kiss to the dead woman, and from that open window, peeking above its three potted geraniums, discern the young woman lying across the bed with her head hanging and the man busy with the murmur of that kiss that uncovers the young woman's throat cut as if from a scar: during the entire time of that decision, which was suspended in myself and preceded that act without ever making the gestures that could accomplish it, for all that time or simply for an instant I must have been imperceptibly asleep.

For the action of that sleep to have been so explosive as to solidify an act by thought alone, the space granted that inexistent beast must have grown, and it must have been there for a millisecond as I was turning away. Since I wasn't able to settle into sleep in that uncomfortable position, all the power of my slumbering body abruptly turned me over, and sleep pushed up towards my face a lighter arm that I'd been crushing beneath my weight, and whose torture was suddenly ended.

I was thus that body fighting alone against a point of pain. And suddenly my body had banished that pain far away into the night where it was pushing me and into which that last chain had barred me from falling. Were thus that twisted arm and that poorly calculated pressure the extension of day, the persistence of an unfinished action that continued in the light, a confused remorse, an unfinished thought that was still roaming wordlessly and without an object, touching the only live point of an isolated limb?

All of the world's sleep must have been that action which I did not see, or, while I was watching, it must have passed behind the world, and for a single instant, moved to the other side of the earth: it must have been taken in a diamond body that blinded its image in me.

And so I saw the fatigue of the man seated on that bed like a dog, and the glowing young woman, and I heard the wounding words she was saying to the man with her phonograph voice and its high-pitched shrill, and with my eyes I caught the shining steel blade of the paper knife that had fallen on her dress and that could only add to the woman's radiance. I was thus the fatality and the unfinished synthesis of all this. And I fell asleep on that bed because the body of the crime had already passed into me. Such dozing off and instantaneous sleep didn't relieve any fatigue or tension: as I entered through the window I discovered that if the "bitch" was dead, that death was the object of an *additional murder*; via that new angle and the frame shot from outside the window, the murder was never deliberate; it *occurred in the past* and in an unpredictable time through which I couldn't add anything to the images.

But that unfilmed scene of the death of the "bitch" must have continually varied the possibilities of a phantom action within me, such that I could suddenly discover that the cadaver *had* to be on the image of the dead woman.

Has the invisibility of a first cadaver of my memory made a continually unexecuted murder the hope of my life, that is, the hope of changing the very sequence of nights? Is this, along with the calculations of such delays, how the world began and how it perpetuated itself in us through the interruption of images? Is this why it is impossible to describe, and why its center is invisibly enclosed in each of us, like the point of gravity of an unknown body? And doesn't the mute certainty of carrying that point shut up like a sacrament maintain the existence of the world in our solitude? and in a time without images?

But prior to its birth, didn't we accompany this deliberation with the representation of a life in which we could have no faith, a life that struck us or amused us like a comedy of manners where stereotypical or incredibly outdated characters found no echo? They were waiting for that moment of truth that could abruptly touch the script that had remained invisible in us. The images that I evoke here are insufficient to lead to such an upheaval. They must therefore contain an anterior knowledge of *what we were awaiting without any hope for it.*

That anterior knowledge has no object; it does not apply to things: it is their entire awaiting, and thus cannot be figured. "Knowledge" is thus not an appropriate term. And yet something does wait for the image simply so that its effect might be cancelled, because, for example, something like the shimmering of the image might disappear: or because the scenes that are composed through the set of images (how they are linked and their isolation, as if, in our memory, an incalculable time separated two tableaux or two shots) fall outside the narration of the film that I was going to provide: ultimately they remain enigmatic, that is, their figuration is not made explicit by what they designate nor by what they cease to signify.

So that knowledge is not exactly mine (it isn't exactly my creation). Rather, it is my alliance and my complicity with forms, with the suggestion of matter that would be specific to those forms that for the most part I do not notice—they each have a quite particular immobility of meaning. And yet I burn them through the full consciousness of that narrative that passed through them like a labyrinth and that will transform them into supplements of that very narrative. All I wait for or expect from the image is its duration and its disappearance: isn't movement also the movement of sense? Despite it all, it's that *the world passed through there*. I don't expect the hand resting on a table and sweating like a face to signify, but to *pass*, that is to say to no longer be a hand. Or simply to *have resembled*, in sum, I expect that the indecisive signification that made it appear will carry it away or change it in my eyes.

And I also expect this because I suspect any object presented as a close-up will not to be recognizable, or will belong to another body than the one it is detached from. But also, if that object is isolated by a frame, or through magnification, I expect it to make a certain disproportion of the world sensible, a disproportion that does not designate things, but rather thoughts and intentions. And the first elaboration, or the first shock of a close-up immediately shows me that even the most insignificant object is my size, and that in such a world we might just have to fight with that, with those forms of increased dimensions, if a new scale of images does not come to correct them. A child's first impression, but also the first indelible truth, is that such a world, swollen at times, urgently threatens to be larger than they are. To halt their growth? To diminish their body? Mostly to invade the world with intangible images that are nonetheless as hard as steel. In sum, through the inalienable newness of that experience, it threatens to make a fissure in things that resemble each other, because these new images—which remain well attached to their image consciousness—have sneaked in a doubt concerning the world (but not through their degree of "reality," their entire reality is the creation and coloration of affects). That doubt does not touch the form of the world, ascertained by the most difficult mastery that we exercise within it at all ages, but occurs because an abyss of supplementary time—the very first—was opened by these images. *That time is not linked to our life.* Nor does it have a mysterious independence. It is not enclosed in any pages as our secret, in the way a possible time exists without simulation in the novels that we keep in our bedroom.

How can one "get one's bearings" in these spaces (to determine the reasonable situation of my body: this is not a simulation of objects that I am busy seeing, it's a cenesthetic affection)? How, for example, can one stop the confusion, or the impossibility of seeing whether a plane is vertical or horizontal? This disorientated world is exactly unlearned, disappropriated. My attempts at appropriating space are guided by proportions, reliefs, unusual flights: the world is constantly exploring us, not only does it explore the entire knowledge of my body, but it explores that body larger than mine that will never have to fly, and will never have to scale steep cliffs with so few perceptions, and so few sensations. It explores that body that lives but momentarily and has a privileged link to the imagination of movement in sensations. I don't know those sensations from having ever felt them—I've never flown over the Amazon using the power of my breath, I've never shot through the sky like a rock—and yet the beginning of these movements abruptly begins that amalgamation of a body with the consciousness of images through which I am then the entire novelty of these sensations; it's only later, or after a very slight habituation that these images appear (*figurent*) for me, that is to say, that they describe or trace the movement of something that is constantly appearing outside of me.

Does this explain how these affects remain experimental, that is to say, how I am a field of experimentations and also the witness of a constant and constantly changing measurement?

The reality effect isn't born of the illusion of a perfect resemblance or simulation since we never lose the consciousness of this approximation. Rather, it is carried on the reality of an unprecedented time that constantly credits those very images.

The anteriority of knowledge (that knowledge, for example, through which we saw the death of "the bitch") is perhaps simply the burn that I add to the image while I am waiting for it to stop, that is, to be replaced by an immobile image. Is this to say it would touch within us a state of the image through which those images, and the time linked to them, would no longer flow in the same way? Or is it that the film can only pass beneath my eyes, or before me, because I know it will disappoint my expectation? I know something will not come, but I am here to wait for it; I wait for something to come through which I would no longer accompany the movement of the images by burning them immediately and in advance (these are sequences of animated images; this, as an effect of fear, is what accelerates a small life of time when I watch them). And so I wait (and the film passes in the acceleration of my affects) without predicting what its form, its contour and its duration would be, an ultimate image: I wait for the resemblance to come. And yet, doesn't all cinema, and every film, more or less, tell me a secret of movement: the act of resemblance has already occurred, you won't see it, only a story will remain, a story whose many ensconced scenes will have to be untangled such that the memory of the film will be neither the memory of the images, nor exactly that of the narrative structure that passes through them.

But, in sum, this anteriority through which I know something imponderable, through which I can no longer feel the weight of non-represented actions, is it not the lack of inheritance of the world that we experience here through an unspeakable malaise, and to which perhaps, in the intermittent consciousness of its suspension, we are nonetheless burning to return? Won't I, instead, and constantly, shut off the world through the pretext of these images, for they do not simulate it, nor do they remain easily and unequivocably within me? Will I not witness all that time for which my life and that of all others does not provide the spectacle, since my most solitary life, or my life as it is most shared with others, garners its strength only because it makes that spectacle impossible. All my life's memories are simply durations of images, slightly corrupted and blinded in part by that black spot that represents my past presence in them, or the abutment of my hope of having been there and being there still; images that are constantly unfinished by that indissoluble link that I call *my* past, I am only ever in them like a back constantly turning away from their light. The time attached to all of this, unless constructed in a novel (in the invention of duration through which the invisible link that sustains and exhausts my images disappears), remains completely invisible. Does all this rise to the surface only through the memory of what I did not experience, and only because perfectly framed images will compose memories that are less, or differently corruptible? Because this time, uncorrupted by my shadow, will be my fundamental knowledge, here in this movie theater? Relations of duration, and of image variations express themselves within me. I am neither quite the site nor the instrument of that thoughtful synthesis, because it's what I'll remember of the film, or what I'll try to say about it. I am the experimental fringe of that new science; I am entirely the instantaneity of knowledge I don't know, also because it's the least figurable. This is what I won't say, because I'll immediately forget it, and attribute it to the sublimity of the film, its vertiginous horror, or my emotionalism. I simply forget that if the newness of time endlessly becomes less than a spectacle, I, myself, am an abyss. And we still corrupt what we call the "images" of our past, we corrupt all memory of our presence because we mix with them, more than our improbable image, the infection of time that we are nonetheless, and to which this past no longer resists: it becomes invisible.

We get the feeling (is it personal, shared?) that narrating a film presupposes we must be able to leave those depths—incommensurable, and without probability—where something occurred (but was it the film rather than I?). It's not really that the film drew something on the screen of our consciousness, or made a step or pointed an index finger toward "another scene" (a scene we don't reach, and not because no image quality exists in it); rather, it's that what the newness of the image touched, and which we could compare to the ignorance of an old pain, did not exist before that film, or before that specific image. Such and such a person, in whom abruptly shuddered a new content, perhaps did not fatally possess the structure of that content a minute before. We should therefore explain why it isn't isolated limbs of sensations that are experienced here, but rather why endless adolescences fatally, pathetically or terribly come to pass.

There is perhaps in all of this one single comical illusion; it's the correct answer to an absurd question: "how old is the spectator?" (The one who claims with shame or pleasure the fact that he is easy to please). It is a perpetual adolescence, an age where nascent actions teach a destination malaise of the body thrown towards them, an infinite age where we experience the destiny of not being able to come to pass, that is, of balancing the world. It is the perpetual age of a young Narcissus, separated from childhood simply by forgetting his first bread, endlessly splitting away from childhood, as if through a suspension of knowledge before adulthood, through that new insipid bread. Strangely enough, burlesque cinema feeds us that old food, slightly augmented with our forgetfulness.

And yet I know through an invariable conviction that none of these ages will return in me, that I will never be affected by an "olden days," or by that uncertainty of bodies that I can barely claim, or by all that time that is prolonged outside of myself, and which accumulates into something that is confusedly experienced and rejects all of this in an endless adolescence already touching my adult body through a porous partition— I know, with a knowledge that cannot lessen with age, via my incomplete memory, via those memories of images without duration, and via those images that grow obscure only because *I have been there*, I know where I endlessly learn that I'm an exception to time. The cinema, and the films I see, provide this additional conviction: I am a fatality.

How does this give me the exorbitant power to watch a childhood? How does this give me the power to contemplate a childhood, and cancel its most inalienable qualities? Is this the secret through which we knew, in that slight anteriority clinging like a shadow to any act, and through the same unchanging certainty, that that woman, that *bitch*, had died before our eyes? Was it through the same anticipation, the same sudden revelation, that yesterday, on another screen and almost in front of me, without me touching, breathing, or hearing it, yesterday, nonetheless, it was a lake?

If this is not the case, any image must therefore initiate a new knowledge, it must comment on its universe, and that human, invariably seated far away yet walking within the image, must be thrown like an obsessive action into the probability that is simply the color and the color of affect whose images are provided "even before" they represent any human action.

It is as if all conduct, all action and all of their causes would necessarily follow from that inflexible steel thread.

But do these movements and threads of reasoning come entirely after the fact? While watching, I wasn't conscious of all of this; yet I retained what follows: by being that strange real hub of the image, I am the instability of its reference nonetheless.

So I am the single fatality of the only possible knowledge that is unfaithful to it. But is this its infidelity, in truth?

Something in the light of the filmed images allows them, not to be identified, but to not be differentiated—that is to say, something loosens the continuity of the film and retains, as in a shipwreck, a few scenes which frame my memory without any of my presence in it; a few past images—which immediately entered the past—on which I leave no stain, no trace of soot; images to which the soot of our body does not adhere.

We don't experience limbs of sensation here—a while back, a second ago. Instead, we experience the entire body of these sensations that has passed onto us like the light from which the images break away, like the vermin of ancient bodies, images splitting away them from in endless points, continuing the exhaustion, breaking the light up into flakes. This consciousness and powder don't reach us; they don't affect us, therefore, in that way.

THE WHEEL OF IMAGES

Are we here like characters in a painting, ruled by the visible of which we might be a more conscious part? Nobody desires or hates anybody on these images, there is no expression of such feelings, there are only gestures and pressures of the gaze that simultaneously occur on screen and within ourselves as if we were their secret. Such attitudes of desire, their destination incomprehensible to our childhood eyes, placed upon this entire spectacle of the coveting of bodies the sensible skin and the imagination through which the possibility of bestiality was revealed in our midst, that first alliance, certainly originating from that cinema (which we would only grasp by chance, already in its full awkwardness, its adult awkwardness), of a heavy gaze, of that mysterious sly look that covered and veiled a woman's face, and which stayed hidden from us by a scheming of bodies (staying that perpetually clandestine scene in the spectacle of desire)—we did not receive their expression but instead the matted quality, the full pulsation of details and the simultaneous revelation that an animal world telling the truth about our own—a truth hidden from our eyes—was suddenly breathing. Take, for example, the fusion culminating beneath our gaze of the adolescent in *Los Olvidados*[24] staring at a woman's sweaty breasts or at her dress with the hallucination of meat in which the desire collected in the woman could not be resolved.

Is the close-up simply this: the childhood unreachable by the expressions of passion measured by objects quartered beneath our eyes? Or the childhood that recognized by its incessant tremor only those passions without an object, like its own fear? And why did that fear awake as excessively and as madly, as madly out of control as laughter? If not because we were then closer to death, and to the fear of dying, because we'd just emerged from it, not because of the unfinished war, but because of our fear of the dark that was just coming to an end; the darkness that had scared us when we didn't know how to speak: we were barely emerging from inextinguishable death and the dark was returning to reveal those expressions of desire that we could not understand, except, perhaps, through a backwards leap. Yet there was nothing behind that jump, nothing behind that leap. There was nothing behind us. We hadn't yet lived; we'd simply been scared, protected, or soothed: as far as we'd been able to flee, we'd only been protected in our fear. We were still so close to it, and its disproportionate scale was surely still within us.

But was this why the expression of desire that we couldn't translate, that seized us in that act of fascination, of giving up, and of avowed brutality between two characters (the kids' mother clinging to her rags, the enameled bowl in which she washes her breasts, the adolescent who smokes like a man, the military blankets on the children's beds, on those shared beds, and the idea that everyone is hungry)…Was this why, through our incomprehension and yet total grasp of the odors of that scene, something remained hidden there like some scheming plot? Why did it all signify "better to die," and in that dim light, with the unbelievable slab of meat waved in the dream of that woman, why did I pass through death unwittingly towards the sun?

That matte quality of the surface of desire did not encounter our ignorance: it reinforced the night.

Memories that are, in sum, all happy memories, that is, separate memories that haven't amalgamated with the rest of the world making our life or the greatest part of our life an obscure transition within it, and in which the world, as past, hasn't constantly remained—thus guided by those surface returns where faces and gestures disappeared through the pronunciation of fateful words suffused with solemnity, importance, or responsibility because people were erasing themselves in them. And the importance, the decisive appearance of those words could not be transported into our life and produce that same effect of a slight murder of the characters in front of whom we'd have pronounced them. Because you could repeat to your heart's content the phrase "anybody got a match?" while throwing a matchbook that nobody could have caught in mid-air like Lauren Bacall without something going gray, or the shot changing, or a cigarette being lit by itself. Because those words "does someone have a light," or "light," would not have determined any destiny, would not even have initiated any encounter because I'd already met long ago those to whom I could have spoken them, and to say the truth, they were already the only witnesses and the only familiar outside to that perpetuation of hachured nights, of long childlike muteness, but also the only constant reason for which the world wasn't a tragedy (because there was that table, that living room, and our bedrooms separated from the living room by a dark hallway, for example, or because there was food surrounded by prayer, by the prohibition of touch, and by ordered ruled for its consumption); because that was the theater where outside actions no longer had any weight, and where dreams ended up cancelling themselves out.

But all of this besides which memories that were otherwise separate were beginning, that is, happy memories that did not prescribe anything about the rest of our lives, and for that reason were only troubling if they opened in the semi-conscious life of that theater an abyss of time that was impossible to fill and to formulate (and if those images and that time were the only permanence, through the repetition of a familiar theater, of which we were incapable)... all of this was beginning to belong to us, up to the repetition of those images of films unbelievably dictated from their world without thickness or color, through their incomprehensible nature even in the many gestures of the burlesque. Since we were missing the very milieu (the light world, the world defined by gray diagonals) in which we might enact those gestures on ourselves, and since, in a child's imitation of a cowboy, of Hercules, or of Robin Hood, those races, those gestures made by limbs that were too short, those horse rides turning in circles awakened no decisive speech, did not stop the wind, or delay snack time, did not outline any sphere that might have represented them as decisive acts. They only ever held a single child barely hallucinating from their repetition, their variation, or their succession, and who would pace around in that courtyard as if he were trying to shut himself into that crystal ball—that is to say, continuing these undoable acts that cinema held close, the child would run out of breath with those screams, those gestures which, since they did not reach the world, could still have reserved a small space for the child in that parenthesis of time through which Zorro, since physical causality had been suspended, could reach the roof of a house in one leap, or with a flash of his sword, topple like bowling pins those same soldiers who had attacked him ten times before.

But all of this, which encountered no outside and no perspective, which did not encounter any responsibility except for a few fugitive resemblances (the upstairs neighbor walked like Charlie Chaplin, another person knew how to pronounce "in the great solitary and frozen park" like Jouvet yet did not make the sequence of *Un carnet de bal* arise), these images without exterior repetition, without any copy in time (not even by that child who'd turn in circles as if he were on a horse, foreshortening all the space around to perform the demeanor of filmed heroes in succession), did all of this invariably begin to enclose itself, to swim in the back of eyes, and less to compose sleep than to belong to us in the most invisible way? It had to be that such happiness was the consciousness of a delay of the world on the action of images, since we experienced another isolation and election in those images, and since they were beginning, perhaps one layered upon the other, to shut themselves in us around an unknown center that we could not reveal, like all secrets, because these images were common to us, because thousands, millions of children were this (Pinocchio's whale, Bambi in the forest, Charlie Chaplin on the horizon), but if this were possible and inimitable, if this possible and inimitable world were able to pronounce its words silently within us (like a melody we would have heard and that we'd sing internally without being able to make it audible): it was thus necessary, through the same fatality that left the world untouched, that these images became enclosed in us with their substance and their qualities safeguarded, like a crime to which we were at the same time the silent witnesses, the actors, and the objects, that is to say the entire duration. Thus, this was simply the first delay of the world, or the parenthesis that gray or very rapid actions opened in it, but for us who were already so far from it that we did not understand that we were not granted this repetition.

The flash, the back and forth, the entire night falling like thickness and a simultaneous assent of desire in the scene from *Los Olvidados*, none of this surprised us, none of this distanced us from anything since we recognized it. Suddenly it brought us closer to a complete matte quality and a dampness, to the request for the dampness of these images, closer to the entire perception of a breath that all of humanity might not know to take, and also through that scrap of meat that didn't seem edible, held in the dream of that woman floating between children's beds, to the suddenly unreal weight of all sleep, and at the same time, to the extreme whiteness of our pillowcases.

If this were to remain, the world had to become indescribable and the part of ourselves in which this consciousness was revived as an image—but was it the most criminal?—had to be attracted to and as if absorbed in that crime without action.

But was this destined to remain eternally suspended until those few images (in my idea not to write a novel) unleashed a childhood, or the imagination of a childhood so imperfectly linked to those same images?

A new matter suspends itself, spreads beneath this shadow of past bodies like the floor of a cathedral tilted "to the level of our language" by confessions and by the search for a time that would no longer bind anything in us except what we call memories through a weave of images, or sensations linked with past feelings—and perhaps those affects might return first *as* images. The weave preserves the full pleasure of hallucinating in our most common memories (at the time, we were millions of children walking through that forest, watching puddles, being afraid of thunder) as our most unalienable secret. These childhoods would be most banal if they hadn't had to fight, to lie, and to ally themselves with adult worlds that alternatively overshadowed and illumined them. Why now can they unleash themselves through hallucinations that return as if at will? Through that slight wavering of film images that do not recompose an entire film or make up the entire duration of a story, but immobilize themselves definitely in their truth. All we know is that we've seen this, as if the unwinding of film reels and the way they settled upon a detail were reruns of time, and testified to this by accruing in our memory their thousand spots and flakes into rock formations, into a rolling of our ages into one single reel on which dramatic, burlesque, indifferent and interchangeable scenes were "edited" (as if in the midst of all of this); as if the greatest transparency of a childhood were revealed here, and not its content or its light.

And yet the film that I saw yesterday has already rejected its first spectator's sequence of positions (that spectator I was when I viewed my first films). It simply kept going, or drew out the obstinacy of the one who doesn't grow old in the same way, or sensibly in the same time, who repeats his beginning, who has not understood his beginning in foreign images. And the film I saw yesterday is already for the most part submerged in an adolescent surprise. Could it return my adolescence to me, or stabilize it? It simply makes it more transparent on those images, and separates it from all the time in which I probably existed (it doesn't contain the desire or anger of that age but only the calm that held them up); continuing to hold it up without making it last, endlessly interrupting it—it thus repeats the same unaccomplished waiting.

In our imagination, these film sessions were like a bath that might regenerate a past being without promising or reserving any future for it.

These images must have only ever taught that "slight anteriority of time" on the unfolding of all actions. In the end, like the murder in *La Chienne* or the end of Dreyer's *Vampyr*, all action must already have *eased* once we witness it. Take, for example, the people walking along the road whom we pass in a truck in Ozu's *Late Spring*. They start to run with some delay in view of the triggering of action we'd anticipated. They are therefore really running helplessly, running as if through wool, moving backwards before our eyes because the two heroes perched on the back of the truck make us glide like wind over the road, carrying us away in the basket that eases within us that time articulated in the disorganized march of the pedestrians strewn along the road, and those two heroes immobilize with the bending of a knee the silhouettes that are now a long way off and who'd begun to run without canceling that fateful delay of a decision and a beginning of movement which was their entire destiny, for a single instant, through the acceleration of those steps that were distancing them from us at a growing pace.

Rather than accountants, we abruptly and immediately become the very passion of that time, that is, its renewed experimentation. We become its perpetual vocation, perpetually surprised. We are therefore at the same time the unconsciousness of that passion, because we believe that its objects—as if we could say the "objects of time"—exist in their place. We believe that they practice in the film or on the backdrop of the screen.

And so the horror film, by emphasizing the object of that new passion, calls out in us that unconsciousness of time. The monster is not a part of us, or the strangeness of our resemblance with an exaggerated object; it's the atom of cinematographic time. We don't know if that atom is us, our foresight, our anticipated knowledge of all events, or our expectation before any event that will prolong that now visible atom. At first that expectation and that event occur through the monstrous body without affiliation; it doesn't completely answer our expectations. Instead, beyond all hopes, it's as if that strangest body was our self, here. It is our self (those shreds of cloth, that mummy, that body tampered with by animals who can't live together according to the laws of the species) or that atom of our self that ignores the only parcel of time that resembles us, and that doesn't flow like all the others.

Does the same thing occur when we try to describe a painting without being exact? And when through that inexactitude something *becomes visible* of what the figures cannot be reduced to? And is this, perhaps, the part of our time that we add to it? That we add in it like the figure that was always missing?

THE WHEEL

In Dreyer's film, the millwheel turns, and flour quickly buries the vampire trapped in the mill's hourglass-like bagging room.[25] This—and the hope that he will be smothered—is our expectation of time, that paradoxical suspension, which has been achieved in the film. The heavy cascade of white powder, even as we watch it entomb the silhouetted figure, seems simultaneously to lift and suspend it in this "flour"-glass, as if it were lifting, making all that cascading powder fly. The flour continues to paint the black man white in his grillwork cage, even as we wonder why it doesn't flow out between the bars (as if the cage were an aquarium, or as if the bars let through nothing but air); the gears and pulleys work like an apparatus of time to produce the disappearance of a body into dust.

And still as he vanishes we experience—just as we do in relation to that mangled floating meat in Buñuel's film[26]—a delay that is located precisely neither in the film nor in us. Certainly it is not the simple effect of brusque movements or shifts in a tableau vivant. And it really only manifests as a delay in the instant of that shift, perhaps because such a stasis *could* have been the fragility of a memory that had already "solidified" before our eyes: so it was also an immobile consciousness. Time lingered over the whole scene as mere suspicion. And indeed it is, so to speak, out of time that the suspicion is generated that falls upon those various universes—through clues or marks that have fallen like alien bodies on these same universes. They don't figure forth anything certain, and of course that's what's so disquieting; we have no clue whether they will finally die, or whether they're caught here as some sort of figure of eternity. Unlike the bodies that appear on the screen, these things cannot at first be detected. Thus the machinery and the flour in Dreyer's *Vampyr*: all we see are the shadows of the wheels. (And I didn't know, being so young—we didn't even know how to find our way in a city—that we were already wandering between continents. What were these languages, these landscapes, and who were all these people?...)

Locked in images are races run against time (locked into the sequence and passing of images), and it is as if the very rotation of the reel's pivot momentarily discovered, by extending a length of actions, that linear representation. Or almost linear, like a squirrel on its wheel, endlessly fleeing its cage, as if he were reeling off, with his galloping paws, the speed that keeps his silhouette almost immobile, arrested in the phases of its movement. We watch the flickering spokes eternally superimposed upon the squirrel's own image. It's pretty much as if this frantic race against time (during which the animal every so often seems to climb, slightly, up the interior of the wheel), in the enclosure of its own mad immobile race and the invisible motor that makes the cage turn in the other direction—as with the illusory effect of a stroboscopic disk—produced nothing more than the perhaps flip-flopping image of the cage as it revolves or limns the incessant spasms in which the animal wears itself out

Thus, before our eyes, in a terminal delay, dies Dreyer's vampire. He dies as the motor effect of multiple images of time, of time's matter and mechanism, which is to say of time's imagination.

Picture a film of a Roman chariot pushed to full speed—the charioteer gripping the reins, the frothing horses pounding and hammering the ground, the sands of the arena, the pavements and flagstones of Rome—a film that shows us, at the thundering height of the race, the virtually immobile image of a single spoked wheel, and the slight oscillation of its glinting surfaces sweeping back and forth across its circumference. Then the shift, the sharp turn, and the apparent collapse of the spokes as they suddenly seem to turn in the opposite direction of the movement of the wheel and make the chariot disappear from view—though the horses do not cease to storm, hurtle into the wind, and torment the ground. For a fraction of a second, the image of movement, as if it had yet to be compounded with speed, is no more than an oscillation, a sort of hesitation superimposed upon the image of this pendular moment (as if the beam fixed to an axis between our eyes were reversing a movement and not a speed). And in the slight exaggeration of the stroboscopic effect, movement seems to become detached from speed—perhaps because the images might only retain the analysis, as it were, of the very slow movements of the horses or the charioteer because they have no proper center, nor can they cancel each other out in their acceleration around an immobile axis describing some sort of circumference. At this point, we witness speed as if it were crossing a threshold beyond which movement were but the recording of a body's phases and positions, or like a wheel detaching itself from a chariot, detaching itself from movement and rendering in slow motion what appears a spherical body striated with beams of light. A bit as if we were seeing it as a round mirror frozen in momentary regulation by the rotation of some sun, equally flat and diametrically opposed.

It's a bit like this image of a body detached from movement itself, capable of being perceived only at great speed and yet which still produces the illusion of a recording of speed: in almost the same way Dreyer's vampire dies before our eyes, captured simultaneously in the movements of the mill's gears, in the cascade of white powder (in the carcass of a beetle tumbling through the sand of an hourglass), and in the silhouette of a squirrel running madly in its cage. He dies at the center of this machinery, like a hand falling off a clock-face. He dies because time suddenly begins to count him and kills him as it is winding down.

All that is necessary, then (is it the same illusion as that of the wheel that can only represent speed as the immobility or hesitation of a rotation reversing its recording, just like the recording of the movement of a planet, in the midst of bodies, hectic or rushing to their fall, showing the only geometric figure resisting the illusion of movement but also so much like an eye—the eye of a hurricane or a dust storm—that watches us in a primordial silence?) is that time begin to count a single body which can no longer represent it, and then enclose it in its apparatus for it to die.

It's thus something like the womb and index of time to which the vampire's body has adhered. He has become, through less fluid matter, the glue oozing from this clock (as the wheel suddenly turns against itself).

(The same wheel on which movement faltered, halted, and resumed, appeared to us as the genuinely mysterious object that cinema could reveal, for there was the enigma: that speed could be held immobile before our eyes as long as it took for us to understand it, certain as we were that in such a scene the stroboscopic disk was the only thing to watch.)

Here, then, is a mill with the wheel turning inside. I can't see the entire house, half of which is submerged in water, but against one of its walls there is an apparatus of paddles that churns the water, as if it were here that the machine's real mystery lay, inverting or lifting the water current through the house. Nor can I see the agitation, the foam beneath the wooden planks, or the transparent cream that swims and winds along the stones (this vessel of cemented stones, damp and motionless, allowing the water by means of the screw propeller to pass into and filter through itself where it becomes light, and flour, and dust as if billions of seconds condensed into the buzzing of insects and, panting and twitching, deposited layer upon layer of the same white powder).

As if these rays of light, along which climbed this very fine particulate dust (that they can touch, stir up, and set spinning at incalculable speed, at once slow and hurried—the mass is ponderous, while the individual grains within it dart about as if panic-stricken, as if each one had been beheaded and left to scramble about in its own private chaos)—as if this powdery beam, thin as a leaf or thick as a pillar, in its capricious movements, its replotting of the directionality of the grains of which it is composed, were to shift abruptly from ghostly surface to hallucinatory volume—passing among large trees and thick foliage, the sun's rays illuminating the forest and the silhouettes of two young people run though the foliage without a sound, a young man leading by the hand a young woman in a white shirt. They had just been running across the half-shadow of a lawn, moving away from the front of a mansion before reaching the edge of the forest. Then there is the silhouette of the vampire running towards the mill, and, past the door, the motionless machinery, the shadow of the spokes, a chain, the toothy wheels. Two young people running across the grass, away from the house. Someone else enters the mill and sets the wheels in motion. The vampire enters the bagging area, and the door closes on its own, shutting him in (he's behind a portion of grill-work, panels that suddenly become the image of a cage). Then the wheels turn and white powder, at first unidentifiable (perhaps it's a talcum-like deposit from the wear and tear of the clockwork machinery that we're seeing), starts to drop and flow. The two young people are briefly seen on a boat, escaping by water; their flight begins with footsteps, running, and is slowed down by the movement of the oars, as their arms have to row like the gears sifting out a cascade of powder, as the oars pull against the water like the black silhouette sinks in the flour, as here and there all those fleeing movements begin to pull upon the same temporal substance and the end of the flight becomes already and everywhere the same thickening of each and every second. The gears keep grinding, like circular jaws, and the flour begins to *climb* up the vampire's silhouette (he thrashes about as if to fend off a billion white flies). The boat reaches the bank; the couple walks through a forest shot through by sunbeams thick with dancing dust, moving in an atmosphere that is both gloomy and bright. The flour falls more and more thickly, the cascade framed more and more tightly, as if to accompany the final perception of a detail in the process of its disappearance. The man is swallowed up, the image of the cage is at last complete, with a hand sticking out of the flour. Two characters walk among the trees, crossing planes of light, and the light continues to hang and quiver in the forest without aim, bodies traversing it, making it slowly flicker. Nothing lurks behind them now: they withdraw after the stilling of the machine, the last tumble of white grain, and the hand rendered motionless. They set in motion the remnants of time that propel them through the forest without generating any new action and despite the wheels no longer turning (or because a remnant of time that is not covered by any action extinguishes itself here, among the twilit trees and a trampling of leaves).

The disproportionate movement that will grind the vampire down and reduce, like a race run backwards, his eternity to powder, will also let the youngsters, on the action of the powder and its musical accompaniment, draw out time as they wander in the woods. The disproportionate movement or effort that must begin this turning back of time is rendered photographically for us by the fixity of the mill's immense clockwork apparatus. Thus it's not an action that sets in motion and pushes those relentless teeth into one another; it's less an action than a cause, the smallest of causes: the *scale of movement* represented by the tiniest of wheels, a baby cog and the only element to which we could have possessed the key, before it entrained giant's feet here to trample whiteness, without knowing that it opened an orifice of time: that white deluge. And here, briefly, is superimposed the white hair of the aged Liszt: one of the vampires comes upon a young girl who has left the house at night and is sitting on a stone bench in the park. He lingers over her for a moment and then leaps away like an animal, leaving her passed out on the bench. He bounds away like a kangaroo wearing the powdered wig of the aged Liszt.[27]

As if all those races piling up before our eyes produced nothing but dust, could make it rise in that white abattoir and in that whitewashed ward, and contained nothing but wheels, muffled noise, and aging.

As if all action had already been relieved by a pervasive wearing down of all sense of expectation, leaving nothing in the midst of these many movements but a heaping pile of dust.

And this assault, projected like a white mantle, makes those years in which the world was encrusted in snow crumble like marble. And the suffocating silhouette submerged in the flour quietly gives rise (like the sight of a cooked insect we might find in some bread) to the inexplicable comfort that we experience at the disappearance (absent the dark shadow of murder) of this body, this character so alien—and the shadow, enclosed within us reveals in that engulfing its distance from us by attaching itself to a species of temporal exteriority—since, really, this character dies as a body and disappears as a body, not as the result of a crushing movement, but through the movement of slow triggering of the mill's machinery which accompanies its disappearance, as if this death were caused only by an excess of whiteness and consummation of light, and as if it were a simultaneous moment in which the action of the mill's machinery or the theater's clock could represent time through a single exhaustion—as if broken on the wheel.

Because this character dies as a body in the slow blanching of the image, and the pallor that descends (as the return of the Roman god Pallor was the mere color of an affect) is the extent of our relief in being present to this prolonged interment and to measure the disappearance of the very body of fear.[28]

There is a child seated within us, watching all of the wheels as they turn faster and faster and all of the movements as they are set going—beginning with the smallest, because that's what he understands, and the empty churning could only touch a body in a cage through a stream of flour. It seemed to him as if this rain, this arc, and this body tortured indirectly by the grinding of the wheels—the smallest of them already having gnawed through the grain—have built from their images a universe of causes, because nothing told him at first that this rain was made of flour, or of chalk or snow, rather than the natural corrosion or endemic leukemia of a vampire trapped in a cage and in the furor of wheels. As if this death were upheld, and released of all isolated and enigmatic effects that only represented its *pure scintillation*.

So it's not death, not yet the end of death's deferral, but the astounding disappearance of a body inside the image. Like that child, judge and witness of the world, who'd once again taken his palace within us without initially comprehending the full figure of the race in the flour, in that accident, and in that cause.

Yet every cinematic death soothes something in us (indiscriminately, no matter what it plays at), in the manner of an image's ascent that finds such completion sublime. This act that we did not commit adds to our consciousness of a cause we could have continued to hold within us, without acknowledging or having it act. As when a stone falls away, or a window opens up in the image: the act doesn't simply soothe us, or free us from the uncertainty of death always skulking around inside us; nor does it ensure our survival (as if by means of this murder we could still remain within the images from which a body detached without us). Does it perhaps give us a figure for a sense of expectation without an object?

THE HUMAN FACE

Prior to the possibility that something monstrous might arise, a scene from Paul Wegener's *Golem* reveals the hopelessness of the human face and of the possibility of changing, transforming or modeling it. We are caught in the clay rag that the rabbi twists, flattens and slides along the Golem's face (for he despairs at affixing a human image on that being made of rock, and can only pinch the protuberances of the eye and nose like a child playing with a lump of pliable clay who can't manage a likeness of *his* own face). Through that wiping of time that struggles, fussing on clay, with what must come beneath, and imposes the certainty that such a powerless gesture (of excrement resisting being softened and affected, if only for an instant, by a passing human trait—but neither does the monstrous deformity appear in that humid paste) hidden in a basement, the secret handling of a face for a body made of rock is a game and a kind of dress-up of time. For beneath that formless, unhinged mask a finer face is hiding, which the earth, blinding and asphyxiating it, covered from our sight.

We know this—through this mobile paste that is only pliable because of its informal persistence, its crude sketch and its impossible miracle—only because the transparency of the clay slipping under Rabbi Loew's fingers attains that knowledge that despairs of the human figure. This is not the despair of an impossible copy, one too difficult to make or requiring art (and training). It arises because the rabbi downstairs in a secret basement seems to have exhausted the efforts of a life: the effort to withstand this copro-plastic activity the face of which, as it emerges beneath his hands, flings back at him its disgust, its heaviness and its inhuman matter through an excremental weight.

The time enclosed in that basement is quite distinctive (in truth, the basement is the bedroom of a child that contains the memory of a single maimed toy, unfinished like that childhood itself). It only measures a resistance of forms, a perpetual rancor of desire, and the only moment that became image, the powerlessness of expression of all matter. But we don't only recoil at a creator's suffering. Through the transparency of that crime and that offence made on a face, we—like him—learn the endless despairing of all human figures—a lesson endlessly delivered on a foreign object.

Yet that paste doesn't glide and no fingers can pinch it: another substance, another object is being twisted before our eyes without softening or rounding into a smooth ball. By daubing an invisible face, it accumulates folds, that is, signs of aging prior to the appearance of a virginal, neutral or surprising face. It accomplishes all the suffering of its substance.

Such despairing has no object (no otherwise dramatic object) and yet Rabbi Loew's hands, through his strange and violent kneading, and his powerful fingers poking holes into the clay, do not open any orifices in that lump of earth for sight or breath. Those fingers only tinkle on a blind immobile face, trying to keep away the insects—as if touching on that immured face the weight that persists in lengthening, in rotating its unformed mass behind our eyes (as if that single shred of matter were twirling very slowly like thick gas).

That sculpture penetrates without any desire. It is a man abandoned by God who touches the site of the human figure. This is only because he is as abandoned as a child grappling with that immense object, a child whose game will provide the illusion of its completion. Through this scene, we become conscious of that same veiling of the human face that occurs when we can touch its divine nature or its reflection. Those same fingers sink into the clay because a face has suddenly—and up to the weariness of that kneading that cause Loew's arms to drop, as if he were spitting on that informal face—lost all dimensions in this slowly immobile paste. And just as suddenly—through the revelation of the deafness that shines in him, the deafness to those clay punches and slaps—it appears that his immobility or despair stand before him, in the body of that aging man groping searchingly for the orifice that might swallow the clay and its chaotic topography, in that aging man or in a face lit up into a grimace of disgust by revelation—or in that kind of muddy duel where the sludge that disrupts the mirror—the single image—can't be erased or settle down.

The image (in this scene where the script of the Golem could be accomplished, or could end) doesn't show us its form but its mass. This is the only way it can be completed. We are inexplicably seated in the image, and yet we wait for it to come, and for that mass—which doesn't resemble us—to be cancelled or to swell up again. In the middle of the image—as it passes endlessly—we wait for its impossible birth, and for that other birth through which it already resembled us. Like a consciousness or a delay, that passing monster touches the certainty that the resemblance has already occurred—or is it simply our metaphysics? Not that a part of the image would have been recorded, and that we'd be in the delay of that recording, as its inevitable second passage. Instead, we see here through a time cut off from memory. Being in the middle of the image, we are the expectation or the hopelessness of its cancellation. We pass through these images—as if through another accelerated film—all of the affects that can't copy the image, that can't take up or imitate anything of it, that can't subject it to the duration of a more invisible thing, like a mass of affects swirling around those same images without finding any adherence there. We experiment that passing of time in us. Seating in an image, we wait for it to come, cease, suspend itself, that is, we wait for it to resemble in a single moment one last time (that's the sublime), and we wait for it to answer the uncertain expectation that prowls between it and ourselves *as* its body.

It's as if the image only gave us its mass here, not its form, and as if this was the duration of our gaze, the only one possible—through this awaiting that is an action, and which can only be attained through the perpetual absence of the morphology of a face.

An endless war—and an endless voyage unfold here. Once the shadows uncouple, we'll become its theater. It isn't a temporary hallucination. Nothing touches us deeply, this death isn't slated for us, and we are nobody's accomplices. Yet what possesses such power to sit us down, lift us, immobilize us, and leaves us more profoundly indifferent, touching us less than the most sublime music?

When we watch these films, suspended to that single instant, how do we know that any one of them (whether funny, edifying, or terrible) is an intermission and that the war continues behind a paper partition, close yet at an incalculable distance? The war lasts as long as the human species—even if nobody can see it. How do we know there always comes a time when the film bores that hole again into duration, that same suspension disquieted because of a train rumbling into the night with massive sighs of steam, the only train that might have carried us far from the bombs and which we missed while we were sitting here, that train that would have saved us from the bomb shelters in the basement where we sat on baskets in pajamas waiting for the air-raid warning to end, listening for a sound above our heads that wouldn't be the sound of planes, that would be the end of the screening, the end of the lull, the end of the jokes meant to distract us from this strange picnic in a basement, at night, at our age, with blankets, listening to stories and textured voices, faces glistening or slightly swollen, listening to the rumble of the "Fortresses," of the bombs, an air-raid warning, then back upstairs where we'd invariably hear "that was close!," "they got Billancourt!," "it wasn't us this time!" It was an intermission, an adventure, and the heroic panic of adults. I even think there were particular shadows on the brick walls of the vaulted basement, or the light flickered intermittently, and in those moments, everyone eyed the electric light bulb that grew a stronger yellow (later, in a theater, I witnessed the mechanism that lowered the lights, a kind of lever touching copper switches in a half-circle: I fiddled with it for an hour to get the light bulbs to turn yellow). Someone must have touched the electric wires in the night. Did that have any relation to being woken up abruptly, to the "hurry up kids, get downstairs!," to the pause in sleep, dignified neighbors in pajamas and coats, our mother's tone of voice constant in the middle of the worst hurricanes, darkness, wicker trunks, knick-knacks in the basement, shadows, the bare light bulb on a wire that single-handedly provided information on the war like a submarine periscope! This went on for months, and nothing happened during those collective teeth-chattering exercises other than slightly burlesque events in the nightclothes of people going down to the basement. We were waiting with the dark, with shadows, and with blinking light bulbs. We were waging war, and waging the occupation in our pajamas. Our life was there from time to time subject to fatality. We were occupied. We existed at the level of rats. The older ones, the adults, waited. They waited for the end of the air-raid warnings, for the end of the Occupation, for the end of the war, for the end of this rudeness, this affront, this humiliation. This was how we began: first, we were defeated (for a week I thought we'd all been turned into slaves by the head of the passive defense crew who rode his bike beneath the windows wearing a helmet, blowing into a kind of fog horn to let everyone know they had to dim the lights). We took a few extraordinary trips, very long ones; we'd end up dirty, littered with straw in a cattle car where someone was eating an apple. We'd been defeated, that was the reason for the endless trips, the picnics in the basement, the rumbling of planes that were more real than we were, and the whole bizarre affair in which we didn't die (the sham was that we had to get dressed in a hurry to go downstairs and listen to the rumblings of thunder without seeing any lightning strike—of course, we couldn't see the light of events since we'd been defeated). That was how the world began, in the flickering of a bare light bulb. We were never to see the light of events again.

Those pajamas, nightclothes and coats under the light bulb, the packed dirt floor and heat pipes stuck to the wall in large white sleeves like legs in casts, and the temporary settling in a common fear, a kind of rite: did that give us our head start on film, the fact that we used to hear things pass above our heads and shards would sometimes fall quite close? Or did we perform that very specific apprenticeship of shadows and masquerades, and sleep preserved all of it, until now, like humus. The hallway runner, the arms that carried us down swaddled in blankets, the packed-dirt floor, the improvised puppets, games with string, the weak light bulb, the creaking of the wicker trunks and the smell of the dry basement, like an ancient large hollow mushroom around which planes were circling overhead.

Since we were never punished, the imperfect crime is endlessly unfinished. Does it return in us? It prolongs the night; it prolongs it in images. It cannot make those images last: I cannot fully recollect even one single film.

But through what knowledge does an end, a fall, a death precede our expectation? Is it because there is no pause in war? Is it because no gesture on screen ever finishes what it has begun?

Or is it that our hands, our huddling under covers, the board games we played under the shaking bulb could never change a thing, like Rabbi Loew's kneading of the clay. All they could attain was the same despair at ever touching the human figure, and if that basement no longer holds anything, we slough off with a shake the clay that was stuck on the face of these memories. It looks like a small heap of humid earth on that decor, the bulb, the coats, the rickety chairs and the rough floor. After the air raids, we were inevitably carried back up to finish our sleep in beds surrounded with undamaged walls and solid chairs. The children fell asleep that way; the adults whispered. A tornado passed through, a hurricane of noises, shaking: dressed in a rush, nestled in that buried ear, beneath an electric wire, watching our changed faces, the only sign of the gravity of the situation was the adults' fear. All else was in the shadows.

Is this why no film has ever been able to overtake death, no movement has ever gotten ahead of itself, and even if we were told to "get lost!" we'd go there in the hopes of finding another light, or because of that unmoored basement that had begun to wander?

The engendering, or genesis, of the visible is linked to something like this: what we can see are figures and shapes that hesitantly convey affects. We must already have seen prodigious things, but their resemblance doesn't reach this place in front of us. Instead, what comes with a new figure is the renewed world of affections.

We don't have an availability to perception but rather a sickness of the visible. Images (like ancient painting) constitute a strange dressing, a soothing application for this, although we never know where the open sore is—its eye and light open in the visible.

Part of the world is hidden by painted figures, by film, and by what our memory retains of them. I can imagine that this part of the world is invisible.

This is why we aren't faced with a spectacle that would stage something unvaryingly perceptible. The figurative world isn't filled by what it shows but by the definition of what it shows.

We are in that film the realized latency of the image: no body can leap in that filmic space without us feeling its imperfect solidarity with our weight.

The world must therefore have a very particular birth, one that is not perfectly linked to the experience of our motor functions. Through the only possible mnemonic definition, the remotest memory of an image must therefore be separate from any bodily movement.

Some enduring engendering of the visible world, in its past, must turn away from us, or keep at bay in the midst of what is closest, a quality that our eyes cannot represent, nor our ears hear, a quality through which all of our senses remain blocked. One part endlessly stealing away beneath another, we are not simultaneous with all that is visible, and the human world doesn't exhaust itself in a single instant and at the same time, the meaning of the human remains what is most foreign. The reproduction of gestures, that is, the reproduction of movement in images, must therefore betray in our eyes the secret of *the most immobile* species, when we'd hoped, despite all evidence to the contrary, to be its secret (its light, its darkness, night itself, which we will speak of shortly).

Can we ourselves be the limitation of the visible? We are also its infinite opening—if indeed it exists only through the affects linked to it *because* it is a particular form of the great illness of the living.

And yet I am its provisional law. And doesn't the feeling of always arriving late to the spectacle of any film arise from that certainty (and the feeling of bringing to the spectacle only that slight delay which is then added to it)? Because the resemblance has already occurred—and we'd be condemned to ignore what it was. All that is left is for us to be present to a play of actions that will never—again—be able to imitate that resemblance, that act without a copy, without a witness.

Paintings, for example, are painted only on one side, and the part that looks at us turns its back to the world. They turn their back to the world's invisible and thus stake out the boundaries of the universe made manifest by the history of species.

Those particular mirrors do not reflect anything of us, because of our obscenity, because of the obscurity that inhabits the invisible part of our body. What they reflect is something we were barely expecting. They show us what we were not expecting, and it's always the sublime that we were hoping for. It doesn't add itself to us, yet we are its provisional law and its life.

Did these images accumulate as humus because they encountered a memory without experience? a memory that seemed to preexist the body of the child, which it can now grasp or lift in its past?

Did they accumulate because we saw old men and women walking very slowly with the gaping silent mouths of large fish? and because their felt walk was accompanied by a mute lapping and an inaudible smacking of the mouth?

We are walking through a hall hung with paintings. Some are very high up and almost indecipherable because of reflections on the varnish on the canvas which add to the distance of our bodies such that the paintings remain nearly invisible, leaving us with only the memory of a placement, a few colors and a reflection that erases them as we pass… We can see immediately that they are only painted on one side—like that book we read as children, *Le Mystère de la T.S.F.*, where we'd search for the origin of the voices that we could activate by pressing on a dial by turning around the book—the side with no paint, the naked canvas accumulating dust turns away from something that, if no one glances at it, only grows darker. Do the paintings line our perambulation, not to represent or to be witness to the past of our species frozen in such extraordinary attire, but to face the invisible world on their unpainted side, and keep it at a distance from the wound of sight that those delicately figured limbs, or that yesterday's peasants continue to soothe and to keep burning at the same time?

Through exaggerated colors and forms, through figurative excess, and through a kind of extreme bequest in the visible, the painted surface holds us, revives, or calms a wound of sight that we don't know where else to place. Nor do we know what might hold it up, or how it dies, infesting all the space it opens onto and meeting the reflection of a sublime face, or how it exhausts itself in its endless worry, or becomes sacred as long as that face stays within it and lends it memory. And thus the sudden calm of Rogier van der Weyden's *Pietà*, through the kneeling, the closed eyes in the presence of a death that envelops all the characters, and the folds of fabric, begins to radiate in a rainbow and an aurora borealis in the background of the painting that lifts the dome of yellow light and of night blue behind our tilted heads. We walk through such a hall as if suddenly all of the paintings offered to our sight simply the worn and dusty surface of their back side, transforming that same hall into a long tunnel at the end of which, if no shard of resemblance remained there—because of the disappearance of all figures we could have seen that might resemble the sequence of possible (or at least imaginable) positions and pauses of bodies from the past in colored milieus—because in that blind hall the certainty that something had been caught in the definition of the proportion of figures disappeared, and with that, the doubt also disappeared that the chain and fraternity of all men from the past would inhere in such sublime spaces rather than in their unrevealed obscenity. The doubt rises again through that long hallway without images that kills in us the *last resemblance*, turning towards our body, as if through the pressure of a screw, the face of the invisible world, without features and proportions, that the figures were keeping at bay through their back… And yet at the end of this hallway and of this endless perambulation, a light would be turned on to maintain the resemblance of a single human being who might, his eyes turned to face us, still hide the rest of the world behind his back.

And so we always skirt that space and whiteness of the image towards the light of a species that might resemble us. Is it because we've seen prodigious things, like old men and women walking on the sand, and know that those moving images retain not the perfection of those movements, but the intelligence of destiny that inevitably orients that march towards the night? And its immediate understanding, achieved without the help of memory, tips that slippery felt, that sand, and those gaping asphyxiated fish mouths over into the unsteady light that extends the solitary advance beyond death, and fells the very slow bodies dancing on a screen into a tilted ray of light, hesitant and swarming with a thousand spots. As if the solitary movement of the old man leaning on a cane before the ocean could only recreate the solitude of he who imagines having touched the limits of the earth in the incessant fluttering of the photons that devour what remains of his body of flesh above our heads, while with his cork feet and a cane deep-set in sand he watches the slightly convex sea on the horizon and the hissing of the foam breaking at his feet—and in front of that intangible wall where no human resemblance remains, with no memory we immediately understand that he had to cross that same tunnel, to rise above our heads in rays where vermin of light ate away at any remaining flesh, and being relieved of that final weight, in the last instants of his visibility, he sits before the ocean without seeing any image. In the same way Homer died, at the foot of the cliff, facing the emptiness while young fishermen beside him picked out the lice that were eating away at this hair.

Our place, that is, our meaning, is fugitive, but nonetheless essential. I believe (as I've experienced it) that our meaning is linked to the delay, to that kind of fatal delay we have in regards to what we see. And the very order of meaning (if we're not simply the operators, artisans, mechanics or dressmakers who patch up fragments of the world, bits of speech, and isolated testimony to human intelligence or pain like scraps of cloth), or the work of meaning as that hold we have on specific details of human destiny, those most figurative or most obscure details that designate as an historical product what remains in each of us urgently invisible, non represented, and unformulated, or is all of this primarily a bequest of sorts of a time where the labor of humanity in the world does not get represented. And might that time be thus affected not to be able to represent anyone's suffering and work.

Does this suddenly become our shame, and the greatest criminal pleasure we are afforded: that signification, words, and images no longer represent anyone. No one will come through those words and images to demand accountability for all the time that we've spent, for all the time we don't share with others—for example, I write and through that fatality without a cause someone suffers at my side, people die, I continue to write. No one will brandish these rags of paper under my nose to make them represent the abandonment of others, my frivolity, tears, or a despair whose criminal hero I would be. No one will hold out like debtor's bills these sheets of paper that should represent the shame of my life in which all these hours, without weight, or sound, or clock, passed in the shadow of a window and hunched over to satiate this incomprehensible passion, seemingly for nothing, hours spent at the blotting paper on my desk surrounded with vials of ink, with pencils, and books but mostly with an invisible desert. No one will hold out these now unrecognizable exhibits and whisper, "Criminal, they were dying all this time. You must have been pursuing the shadow of that death!" Nothing can convince me that there's a cause here, or that this experimental silence, born as if in the eye of a hurricane, in the coldest center shining in the work and death of others... Nothing can convince me that all of this, through the sovereign lightness of absence, through that implausible detachment from any human figure... that of all this, in a word, is the terrible cause of an unknown crime that pursues and harasses us, stealing away the night and panting within us. Nobody will say it as certainly as I know it—by these images and words added one to the other, by these words that have slipped behind the shadow of a window, I am an irresolute fatality, or the imagination of a lasting instant in the human species. And if I'm here instead of leaping, loving, or answering someone, isn't it also in order to fill a kind of delay? I must deliver something like a life to the duration of that delay and to its impossible exhaustion. Hunched for years over word-filled paper, I don't see, and therefore don't perceive with utmost terror that those pages don't reflect any human face (and certainly none of the ones I'd like to see there) and that what I'm doing in this shadow webbing is simply pushing aside their resemblance. With a single hand, I brush aside the very face of the entire human species, and caught in that basement, kneading those words, touching that clay, endlessly manipulating these images, these gleams and minuscule memories of reflections, I brush aside the resemblance of the entire human species. Nobody will convince this one here of such a crime, since he knows it in advance, yet suspends it, forces it to wait. He is the very life that begs it to delay the final extortion. There's no one else, for it's in the pleasure of that crime that he enjoys his full innocence in advance. And since he's the only one to experiment both *that* innocence and *that* crime, brushing aside the resemblance of the human face, and knowing that he's enclosed in time, in expectation, and in the work of others—to say the truth, the entire world closes off if one single being's pain remains unanswered—there where the human face is nothing but an image, will he be able to reach that last resemblance through which the featureless face, its outlines stretched thin, and that entire world disfigured while his reclusion lasted suddenly begins to resemble what is making it dissimilar, decomposing, disguising, or grooming it without end, changing those very images so that it might be pared down to attain to the dreadful resemblance of time?

And who might hold this thing out to me as representing time, or something else, something that would inexplicably be linked through a single word to someone else? No face can appear in this thing, within this heap, among those rags. Did this thing slowly force a certain inconsistency into the visible that is supposed to exist in the world yet remain unnoticed and taciturn? Did it search for a character sitting in the shadow, throw something at its face, watch its eyes, and, unsure if it could resemble our species, did this thing simply and incredibly cause time to age?

In the linking of movement, in its fits and jerks, we know that all we witness before the screen is that delay of movement. Neither the vampire's death or the "bitch's" death, nor the trembling that immobilizes the spokes of the chariot wheel in its race, nor the Japanese actors running behind a truck that passes them and sends them shuffling on the horizon will trouble or even encounter that same feeling of movement. All of this is certainly powerless to represent our life, or to "replay" any actions in it. If we experience delays or slight anticipations of action here, it's not the represented subject but the sub-stance of time (invisible up to that point) that becomes our knowledge, our pleasure and our entire experience.

Yet if the simultaneity of movement can hit us like an act to which we are freely present, what can we make of the extreme respite of that represented action? (Certainly, I begin by staying outside of the field of the image that I'm watching. Perhaps

I'm virtually the entirety of the field, which I watch without staining or invading it? It must be that the movement realizes a kind of bodily destination, one unknown or not experimented until then.)

If time has become visible in actions, it must be that it is our emotion. And that specific pleasure linked to time must not be its wisdom or its knowledge, for there is no knowledge of time, but instead it is time and pleasure that links time within me and that can, even without having recourse to the representations of actions, link me in it as one of its fragments. If represented actions become in a sense transparent to that duration, to that interruption, to those artifices of succession, my body, mind and memory must be porous to the experience of a temporality that my life and power are incapable of (that is, that they cannot "contain"). In this way, my life and power reveal themselves as suspended to the specific extension of that duration that none of my organs had ever experimented. Is there something, like a soul, lodged in an incessant unknowing of time? Or does something remain within us without causality so as to be suspended when this new time appears?

And do such suggestions of movements, transparent to a new edict of time, encounter, for example, that form of empty action in which—although our entire body is continually busy there—we remain simply porous and as if open to nothing-ness, to dreams, to a rest without images, to a lassitude that does not have the same tension as fatigue, where we simply and without suddenness think of nothing, that is, turn our backs to the world?

Was it an absolute coincidence that a bare light bulb swinging on a wire imprinted that pendular movement or that metronome as an expectation affected only by the power of the light? But that power and loss of luminosity wasn't movement—it was even immobile, as arrested as the rumbling racket beneath the belly of a plane, stunned faces or trees whose branches started breaking off and flying one summer afternoon. If all of a sudden the wire and light bulb were twirling violently in a half-circle, not in order to project swirling shadows on a wall but as if a heavy body were swinging from it, seated in the barren light of the bulb and flinging all its limbs, feet, legs, in spurts and with a movement of the hips, towards the brick ceiling, we understand in a gleam that this image is closing, that it leaves us, no longer a secret, and in that instant when the echo of that strange climax in a faraway night ends, a mute thud strikes something in the middle of our life—through that added eternity, the movement of the oscillating bulb suddenly softens, loses its charted course, no longer emits a sound, and the basement where it twirled stops existing once a young woman penetrates beneath the light, once a mummy seating in an armchair pivots around in it, and once, at the end of *Psycho*, a hand stops the arc of a knife that has already struck; as if that last strike in which we heard a cry were filming once again the gleam of a subterranean space where we had hoped death did not resemble anyone.

And the same time, the same fingers that cannot give shape to the Golem's face, as we can see them, both fingers and face smeared with clay, because they hold to the despair of crafting an absolutely smooth and expressionless human face, and wish to do so as child's play, that is, with a toy that is immediately given over to the confusion and stammering of affects (is this why all children's games keep that excremental twist that would model indistinct affects on their own incomprehensible event, affects that cannot reach any kind of resemblance before the children can master the extreme proximity of their body with that distressing time—is that why such games attain resemblance yet their product remains disfigured?). Doesn't Loew's gaze, adhering to that incomplete doll like a shapeless caress, contain the torment he inflicts on clay with that extreme haste as if, in the instant before it takes on a representation, he were handling with furious kneading the invisible quantity and weight of the human body that cannot be figured, and in the midst of our turmoil, touching that last revelation at the back of our eyes: the body and the copy, or any creature, is completed only through the wound that the visible leaves in us. Or this, the monster is only a monster if that wound remains a wound in our eyes.

But is this action, which is only rarely a cause or an event suspending all effects, common to this intention, or at least comparable to this consciousness of the crime (that is, to the only thought that is simultaneous to the only event in the world) in the midst of which (as if it were the reel recording the now visible action) a woman drops to the ground from a bullet shot in the street, behind the action of a music box, behind a child's fierce resolve, with a move that lifts her skirt, revealing a patch of skin above her stockings as she lies before a broken window: the crime is the power of time to reach, simultaneously, all bodies within it that were splitting off.

How can we see all of this, and see something rather than nothing? Rather than fill our gaze with the absence of a gaze comparable to the absence of thought that periodically occupies us? We could imagine that this would let loose seedlings within us, spinning tops of slowed down grain, that we might see the half-closed eyelids, as in light sleep, the animals still in their larvae, tadpoles of humans (or displaced by the mists in *Throne of Blood* through a loss of proximity in a shot without any reference points, the same two horse riders churning and harassing humid dust). A gaping eye has opened within us; it has birthed the visible and will no longer destroy it. In our experience, the visible doesn't know the sleep of thought. In the same way, it doesn't have the same beginning, and the same stuttering, daily and in every instant. Nor does thought experience that perpetually inchoate act that brings it forth as if from its impossibility, and maintains within in that final impossibility and the utmost limit where it is simply the world's inconsistency, for example. Where thought is a particular way of suspending the sensible, and is also that particular doing that no longer links the sensible such that, for example, its proximity, its dampness or its grain will last nearer to me, yet will not feed my body or affect any of its perceptive organs. If a written flower has no smell, if it does not affect my sense of smell, or awake the memory of that smell, I must therefore produce the duration of an imagination of bodies comparable to that of classical physics. These bodies are not rational; they do not possess the zone of affections that provides a body with a world, that is to say, a solidarity. My thought would thus be constituted by that new solidarity between abstract bodies, just as that writerly fragrance initiates a perception without a body (it will, for example, be linked to a spark, to the evocation of wind, to a thick paste of memory, or through its incomplete description it will remain like an insect stuck to the thickening of my memories).

But that wakening thought, troubling a world at first without objects, and which can be reduced to the imperfect island of that unfinished fragrance—a thought which is perhaps also the hesitant search for a new cause, unknown in all phenomenon—is perhaps the inchoate act par excellence of my entire life, although one endlessly reducible to naught. Nothing is transformed there. These words do not persist. Perhaps they do not allow any other perception to unfold, as if they were addressed to beings only susceptible to being moved or convinced in the memory of their bodies—as if (*because*) the musicality that arose in them, and which entered the world through them, was endlessly seeking a new body that would answer it, as it roamed or turned in the air, as if a single point that was truly vulnerable and still out of reach could be discovered through that kind of floating and the levitation of the body in memory.

That quality, that shift (and the persistent strangeness of affects that touch neither what is possible for the body, nor its imagination, but only its motion and the quantity of motion without organs *as* emotion, thus reaching it not at the site of the real or ideational body, but in an instant of vanishing, as if that debacle were the endless and vain prelude to its reorganization into a new combination), and that transmuting of the world connect what words do within me to what time and atoms, or the most elemental parts of matter—its gaseous state, for example—do in the universe.

Thought knows the genesis of the material universe (where it is attached to an invisible universe), that is, its destructible state, the loosening and spinning of its smallest parts—sight isn't affected by that muddled beginning or by the perception softened by its open wound that is the consciousness and immediacy of the visible.

Only in cinema is sight affected by such a sequence of muddled events. (It isn't a body moving underneath cinematographic images, it's the very definition of the visible, even more than its proximity). Sight is accompanied by its repeated and endless genesis: it suddenly becomes a thought attached to the impurity of its birth—that birth will not leave it, and lets its minute body float in it to define it—but not to the impurity of our presence within it.

Here I see, combined, the genesis of the world (as well as its elementary destruction), the genesis of thought or its slow inchoation, and the beginning of the visible that is not yet a figure or an action.

In Kurosawa's *Throne of Blood* we find gray—vapor, fog, a before of the image. That gray is not an indistinct veil placed before objects, it is a thought without a body or an image. It is the beginning of the world in the middle of a story, like dawn and dusk enclosed in that story.

By thinking on cinema in this way, not touching the totality of its phenomenon or perhaps what is the most essential in it, but naming what is for me its renewed event (and renewed in our memories)—all I've learned is this: in the midst of all that is solid in the world, and of all images, a new substance becomes sensible. This substance grips me, not through the suggestion of actions, or through the repetition of movements, but because it affects the sight—the entire responsibility of the visible—of all the phenomena and the events the thought of which is characterized by their prior-body and their preliminary, incomplete figure. Here, the visible is new because it constitutes an act of thinking (it borrows its characteristics and morphology) rather than an object of thought (it is not a process that can be assimilated or reduced to figuration). Such matter, taken up in a new movement (for the experience or knowledge we have of phenomena) retains the tremor of an inchoative thought but not its product (it is neither elocution, nor writing): it is a world that trembles, becomes dissolved and is reorganized because it *has been* seen, in sum because the definition of the world is affected by a movement.

In a series of shots, the same landscape (hazy, clear, detailed, seen from the top, musical) varies constantly and constantly changes universes. The image of the world is mobile in its details: it does not discover surprising aspects of the same world but other worlds under those aspects.

Why does thought thus affect the form (of haziness, of extreme mixture and of morphological confusion) through which, since it does not belong to the domain of perception, it becomes a body not via its contours but via the middle of its mass by adding something improbable to the definition of that mass (in the scenes that literature adds to the world, or in the new isolation of causes that a speculative thought releases from a body) as if thought and the disturbance of language might add, of their own volition, a new point of gravity that might make the world step into a novel aspect of itself. Perceived in its disequilibrium, this is the same point that Kafka evokes as the only mark and the isolated symptom beating uncertainly in his writing the recall of an ancient body, one that is ancient only because it is always prior to writing (because the impossible realization or the unfinished death of that falsely anterior body would maintain the incessant tearing apart and malaise of that body and that writing in an inconceivable synthesis).

If the world of phenomena, far from reproducing the real conditions of my vision, is thus natively affected or characterized by that new disruption (by that haziness and grayness between bodies, creating new perceptions, a novel grid through which worlds, not phenomena, follow one upon the other, since there is no experience or hallucination that could allow me to know that succession in the time of my perceiving body, that is, in the perceptions that I am constantly responsible for or that I make possible), I know that this new world, not in the manner of a museum of phenomena, no longer surprises me as that very change of perceptions but in the manner of an act of thought. When I am in front the cinema screen thinking I am simply present to actions, as the world is continually engendering itself before my eyes while changing the proportions of the visible, I know that it goes through definitions of matter (such that the envelope of a visible form and its imagination can insistently constitute its substance). I understand this clearly, as I see in Edgar Allan Poe that the unlimited genesis of the universe in its very detail unveils what, in the fantastic, is neither narrative nor figuration but rather an allusion to the constant alterity of this world as it is being born. But if, on the contrary, my though closes off some of my body's perceptions, how does this (a specific close-up or jerkiness, mist in an eye, a fade-out, or the constant slow-motion in a film by Jean Epstein, for example) relate to thought—through a conviction that negates appearances and refutes their objections—or relate only to thought? Precisely if that thought creates a new speech (or a certain quality of speech), and at the same time covers the entire world with a new silence, or just barely reaches that ultimate "supplication of silence." But if this resembles thought, suddenly and from that moment on, it's because the world that opens in this way, through the fatality of a universal spectacle, comes to us (upon us, towards us and as if from within ourselves?) in those spots and in that marbling—as if it were inhabited by an anteriority of our desires that do not recognize their objects—because it is inhabited. For those new appearances—in which we must sometimes accommodate partial objects in order to grasp them, and whose full form and reference we always misapprehend—are *affects*. Those affects do not have faces, they do not yet have names: yet in a muffled way, we consent in them to those strange antecedences of emotions and to that first irrationality that the apparition of figures and actions will complete before our eyes (this is played out, via an undecipherable mystery, in the opening sequences of Hitchcock's first films, *Murder!*, *Blackmail*, *Champagne*, or in the color and space that spread through the credits of Mizoguchi's films). In this way, I learn that participating in such a spectacle does not lead me to the world through vision. Instead, an emotional charge emerges in an irresponsibility of my vision. The spectacle provides the back end or bottom of that vision, it entrusts it to the slumbering of my feelings and of my moral being, that is, to the only duration within me that acquiesces to the meaning of the world.

This is not thought that has become visible. The visible is affected and irremediably infected by the first incoherence of thought (that inchoate quality that does not remain in thought, as a sign of its nobility or its humanity). Or is it that such incipient thought, as well as the visible marred by that disruption anchored in it like a birthmark, are equally—

although they can never cross nor completely abolish the world to which they address themselves, the world from whence they come and whose last demands for rest they bely—an incessant awakening of all of humanity and, rather than hallucinations, an immense, impossible sleep (in the manner of a certain quantity of sleep that would have fallen outside of the purview of the species)? Or does all of this remain an imperfect or impossible spectacle (we are here the fundamental color of the image, just as we were nothing but the sweat of fear in our memories and what kept placing on them that black cover where no face can be recognized).

But, in the midst of the experimental time of comedy, where accelerated affects are addressed to *nobody*, does my nervousness, or that chain or net of unknown feelings that pass through us, awake me suddenly, waking a kind of shame and certainty that I cannot extinguish? For in that very moment there is killing in the streets. In that very moment in which I stupidly witness an American cattle drive the war *does not stop*, massive police forces take position silently and there is killing. And I have no other response than to invoke the dignity of a life, of any life, as if it were already too late. As if that enormous cinematic machine whose reality, whose reel, and whose perpetual movement we are, made all life insistently more solitary by pulling the dead *out of our life* with a repetitive, light, and endless movement as if they were foam. We knew that such intangible feelings (as if some resource for truth were trying itself out through them, and exhausting itself there) that such finer emotions were like light fingers, and through I know not what solidary link were a murderous machine, a kind of wheel, a power to strangle resemblance and the human grimace—before it could signify anything, before it could send any credible sign of distress to those who were watching.

And yet, each human death, that endless line of murders and suicides, each human disappearance eclipsing the incomparable solidarity of that life in the world, leaves an unfinished answer in us, stupidly and gruesomely suspends our own death. The new silence, and the cowardice or fatality from whence it comes, is perhaps simply the weight of that body that has been heaped upon us for an instant.

And yet bodies, their details or the objects that would thus be, through a film scene, taken up in the time that suspends any outside of that scene, are not its ornaments (Can we repeat that those objects, quite particular in what makes them unrecognizable at first, signal or paradoxically locate the anteriority of a world that is opened in us when we await the realization of desires? Can we say this is *already* the case?) If time reaches bodies where they are not simply figurative, and if an invisible chain that capriciously linking scattered elements is pleasure, and if the necessary action of that pleasure is to enunciate or vary together certain objects of its most faithful thought, and if the crime is thus the cause, that is to say, the divination and prescience of a simultaneous distribution of effects and events... What does this result in? It results in a desire that is defined by its realization (as if desire required an autonomous world, or at least a closed one, and its specific work were, while leaving them intact, to devour the objects of this world, to replace them, and to be its affirmation in their stead). It results in a sovereign desire.

This dictates for us an antecedence of pleasure, and that is the only crime. Yet it is anteriority in desire, and something like its obsessive realization, thus implying a kind of unknown causality.

The delay we experience in the representation of actions (in the back-and-forth of their effects) cannot be filled—and the place that a chain of actions cannot fill is part of our experience of that time. Moreover, it cannot be taken in by the ultimate crime that pushes all other crime away from time. And yet, signification is sworn to *represent* it: it is the glow of a single event with which we could not be simultaneous. It is the first resemblance that escaped us (that took place without us), that is, the only announced death that did not occur to us in life itself, because we did not recognize it. This is the theme of Archibaldo de la Cruz's "criminal life." His entire life lies in one single signification or can no longer escape the unfolding of all events in an endless murder, or an incessantly recurring murder whose objects offer themselves up to an impossible satiation. It persists in belying that single torment: that life has no cause.

But what else? The visible is that more sensitive sickness of our species through which time wrests us from figures that disappear from within ourselves.

Or is the species that entire sickness for which, *save time*, there is no innocence: there are only causes.

That delay is thus an image, or a signification.

That delay cannot be filled. Nor can it be taken on. (It is just barely that form of time which is shown to us as a movement)...

Archibaldo's endless crime is simply this: he is the obstinate ignorance of an invariable and constant cause, of the simultaneity of effects, of the dead, of the musical accompaniment of death, and of its "refrain." And isn't the obstinate and involuntary repetition (as if fatally attached to the compulsion of seeing) a doubt about that accidental object, that interior snag and the flesh of movement, the first woman's skin glimpsed through a slip on a hardwood floor that revealed the governess' legs, because only the refrain of death could redo that very thin unveiling that remains therefore the most secret, or redo the very event in which grew concentrated the responsibility of death, with its solemnity. That event consecrated by the entire uncertainty of the crime, and its disproportionate nature.

I knew, for example, that the extreme delight of a glimpse of flesh (that is, flesh belonging to another woman), could be a child's discovery and secret, an emotion of perception and not the duration of something that remained constantly visible; a manner of truth, unique and sudden that colored a silhouette, a voice, clothes and a smell like the secret we would have shared. I hold the hidden secret of that body, and my entire heart beats for it, so strongly do I wish it were sublime in its entirety, and that that single visible fragment were a love note madly proffered to my untried desire. In an instant, that body moves in secret to that place a smile and a kind of new maternity that would be full, intact and very close and for which a child, seated in the undergrowth, would silently roll over in the leaves during a fall afternoon.

In Archibaldo's life, it was the ignorance or the doubt concerning the most simultaneous object (simultaneous in movement, in the gaze, or through hearing) that followed the perpetual unknowing of a first crime: the repetition of that childhood rolled up on that single woman's stocking crowned by a shred of skin.

So it's in a lake, with gargling and that suffocating of sounds, that the refrain of death must disappear and the music box must sink—kneeling because of that song, kneeling before the woman and clapping at length with my eyes locked in hers, I could have clasped the bottom of her dress indefinitely between my fingers and kissed it.

We'd stepped outside, through the large open doors, the foyer brilliantly lit, and into the night that no light could stop, or bring to a halt, or even limn. It was warm out and the rain had stopped, seemed to have stopped for hours. There were stars above, and everything was still turning in my head, and no one was talking. I felt someone touch my arm, it was warm, cigarettes glowed behind me (I'd heard the flicking of lighters and turned to see the flash of faces), footsteps. Nothing could exhaust that night, nothing could fulfill it.

There were scraps or crumbs in my pockets that I couldn't connect with anything. I had no idea how they got there, since I never carry bread that way.* The row of poplars was no longer very far away, and nothing was coming from over there. If it had rained more, we would have been able to smell the dampness on the warm road.

We knew that one of the farm dogs on patrol would start to bark at us once we turned the corner. One of us was walking

---

* Thinking about it today, perhaps if nothing had decomposed there and if I'd felt crumbs like abandoned grains of sand, some time—even the time that didn't connect me to anything—must have fallen through that narrow opening because in sum, without my knowing it, I'd have roamed an instant or a day in that sensible time.

in the grass beside the road so as not to make too much noise, but I could hear twigs whipping against his shoes and the squishing of grass.

If any drops had fallen, I would have felt them plashing against my hand or sliding under the collar of my shirt—we would have run straight to the lane, without stopping, then to the house, where the light would have been abrupt and very bright, and we would have gone to bed and whispered together a bit.

F. touched my arm and showed me the stars she knew by name: the charioteer, the bear. I mostly grasped the Milky Way and the story of the milk spilled there in the night.

Sound of shoes, bodies that were becoming almost visible; voices rose up again in a night that was so perfect that we could barely see anyone. F. showed me the stars, I tried to tell where they were.

And we were there, in the sound of old fashioned shoes and light laughter rippling up from conversations, walking very slowly and grasping hands, for the first time, suspended in that night.

Translators' Notes

1. See Jean Louis Schefer, "Musil," in *Choses écrites: Essais de littérature et à peu près* (Paris: P.O.L., 1998), 289–302.

2. See Soren Kierkegaard, *Either/Or: A Fragment of Life*, Translated by Alastair Hannay, Abridged Version (New York: Penguin, 1992).

3. Michel Delahaye, "Carl Dreyer," in Andrew Sarris, ed., *Interviews with Film Directors* (New York: Bobbs-Merrill, 1967), 112–113. See "Entre terre et ciel: Entretien avec Carl T. Dreyer par Michel Delahaye," *Cahiers du Cinéma* 170 (1965), 16–18.

4. "Take someone dying of an advanced old age: they die in detail; their exterior functions end one after the other; all their senses close in succession; the ordinary causes of sensations pass over them without affecting them." (Marie François Xavier Bichat, *Recherches physiologiques sur la vie et la mort* [Paris: Charpentier, 1866], 110); see Jean Louis Schefer, "Remarques sur un usage du corps," *L'Ecrit du temps* 8/9 (1985), 67–83.

5. Edgar Allan Poe, *Eureka: A Prose Poem* (New York: Putnam, 1848). See Jean Louis Schefer, "Eureka," in *Choses écrites: Essais de littérature et à peu près* (Paris: P.O.L., 1998), 261–69.

6. Robespierre's "lunettes vertes" are mentioned in (among other sources) *Recueil d'anecdotes biographiques, historiques et politiques sur les personnages les plus remarquables, et les événemens les plus frappants, de la Révolution française* (Paris: Du Sault, 1798), 281.

7. Gustave Flaubert, *Bouvard et Pécuchet* (Paris: Alphonse Lemerre, 1881).

8. Erich von Stroheim, *Queen Kelly* (1928).

9. Robert Musil, *The Man Without Qualities* (London: Secker & Warburg, 1953, 1954, 1960).

10. Paul Delaroche, *Les Enfants d'Édouard*, 1830, Louvre, Paris.

11. Frances Hodgson Burnett, *Little Lord Fauntleroy* (New York: Scribner's, 1886).

12. Claude Autant-Lara, "Robe pour Catherine Hessling," 1925.

13. *Duc de Saint-Simon, Memoirs of Duc de Saint-Simon, 1691–1709: Presented to the King* (Warwick, NY: 1500 Books, 2007).

14. The actor who plays Professor Immanuel Rath in Josef von Sternberg's film, *The Blue Angel* (1930).

15. Vittorio De Sica, dir., *Shoeshine* [*Sciuscià*] (1946).

16. Christian-Jacque, dir., *Boys' School* [*Les disparus de Saint-Agil*] (1938).

17. Ben Sharpsteen and Hamilton Luske, dir., *Pinnochio* (1940).

18. Jean Tarride, dir., *Skylark* [*Adémaï aviateur*] (1934).

19. Franz Kafka, *Diaries, 1910–23*, trans. Joseph Kresh, Martin Greenberg, and Hannah Arendt (New York: Schocken, 1976), 391.

20. Kenji Mizoguchi, dir., *Ugetsu Monogatari* (1953).

21. Franz Kafka, *Diaries, 1910-23*, trans. Joseph Kresh, Martin Greenberg, and Hannah Arendt (New York: Schocken, 1976), 18.

22. Novalis, *Notes for a Romantic Encylopaedia: Das Allgemeine Broullon*, trans. David W. Wood (Albany: State University of New York Press, 2007), 115.

23. The French term "expérience" can mean both *experience* and *experiment*. This double meaning is fundamental to understanding the active process of the experimenting of affects.

24. Luis Buñuel, Director, *Los Olvidados*, 1950.

25. Carl Theodor Dreyer, Director, *Vampyr*, 1932. The character of the doctor, suffocated in the mill, is not clearly depicted as a vampire himself in the film (or in Sheridan Le Fanu's novella *Carmilla* [1872] on which it is loosely based), but rather as the vampire's servant. As Jean-Louis Leutrat notes: "Il s'agit d'ailleurs plutôt d'un complice du vampire dans le film" (*Kaleidoscope: Analyses de films* [Lyon: Presses Universitaires de Lyon, 1988], 123). Yet the ambiguities of the doctor's role and of the forces acting through and upon him are considerable. See, for example, David Bordwell, "Vampyr," in *The Films of Carl-Theodor Dreyer* (Berkeley: University of California Press, 1981), 93–116.

26. Luis Buñuel, Director, *Los Olvidados*, 1950.

27. The image of Liszt as a vampire may be inspired by the composer's association with Hungarian folk and pseudo-folk traditions, as well as Liszt's devotion to Byron and other Romantic propagators of vampire legends. There may also be an arch allusion here to Ken Russell's film *Lisztomania* (1975), in which Wagner is portrayed as a vampire who preys on Liszt.

28. Schefer alludes here to Livy's false deification of the personifications of Pallor and Fear (*Pallori ac Pauori*) in *The History of Rome* 1.27.7.

LIST OF PHOTOGRAPHS

Page 26: Tod Browning, dir., *The Devil Doll* (1936)

Page 28: Carl Dreyer, dir., *Vampyr* (1932)

Page 30: Terence Fisher, dir., *The Mummy* (1959)

Page 32: Terence Fisher, dir., *Frankenstein Must Be Destroyed* (1969)

Page 34: Tod Browning, dir., *Freaks* (1932)

Page 36: Frank Capra, dir., *Lost Horizon* (1937)

Page 38: Marcel L'Herbier, dir., *L'Inhumaine* (1924)

Page 40: Edgar Kennedy, dir., *From Soup to Nuts* (1928)

Page 42: Clyde Bruckman, dir., *The Finishing Touch* (1928)

Page 44: Josef von Sternberg, dir., *Der blaue Engel* (1930)

Page 46: Erich von Stroheim, dir., *The Merry Widow* (1925)

Page 48: Erich von Stroheim, dir., *The Merry Widow* (1925)

Page 50: Lewis R. Foster, dir., *Men O' War* (1929), production still

Page 52: Carl Dreyer, dir., *Master of the House* (1925)

Page 54: Tod Browning, dir., *Freaks* (1932)

Page 56: Tod Browning, dir., *Freaks* (1932)

Page 58: Tod Browning, dir., *Freaks* (1932)

Page 61: Unidentified Mack Sennett production

Page 62: Unidentified

Page 64: Unidentified

Page 66: Charles Chaplin, dir., *Shoulder Arms* (1918)

Page 68: Jean Renoir, dir., *La Chienne*, 1931

Page 70: Carl Dreyer, dir., *Leaves from Satan's Book* (1921)

Page 72: Charles Chaplin, dir., *Work* (1915)

Page 74: Charles Chaplin, dir., *A Night in the Show* (1915)

Page 76: Buster Keaton, dir., *Battling Butler* (1926)

Page 76: Claude Autant-Lara, sketch for the wardrobe of *Nana*

Page 78: Jean Renoir, dir., *Nana* (1926)

Page 23: Sergei Eisenstein, dir., *October* (1928)

Page 23: Josef von Sternberg, dir., *Macao* (1952)

Page 23: Josef von Sternberg, dir., *The Blue Angel* (1930)

Page 23: Josef von Sternberg, dir., *Salvation Hunters* (1925)

Page 23: Alfred Hitchcock, dir., *Foreign Correspondent* (1940)

Page 23: F. W. Murnau, dir., *Nosferatu* (1922)

All photographs are from the archives of *Les Cahiers du Cinéma*.